Getting Into Medicine
The Pushy Mother's Guide

Anna May Mangan

Getting Into Medical School
The Pushy Mother's Guide

Spine Publishing, Dr Prep Ltd, CPC 1, Capital Park,
Fulbourn, Cambridge, CB21 5XE

British Library Cataloguing in Publication Data
A catalogue record for this book is available from
the British Library
ISBN 9780955132544

Cover © Toby Morison

Contents

INTRODUCTION

Let's get this out of the way early, I'm not a Doctor or in any way associated with the medical profession. My credentials for writing this book are my twin daughters, Molly and Martha, who recently went through the process of trying to get a place to study medicine. They got places after a long and lively bun-fight but many of the talented sixth form students they met along the way, who also had all the right grades, attitudes and the potential to make brilliant doctors, didn't get a single offer. Making an application to study medicine at a UK university is a test in itself and any potential medic needs to be fully prepared for it.

This is the book I needed when my daughters announced that they both wanted to qualify as doctors. This book, unlike so may others around the medical theme, will focus on *the* central question for any prospective medic and their family – WHAT HAS TO BE DONE TO GET A MEDICAL SCHOOL OFFER? If that's what you need to know – read on.

The idea to write this book originally came from an editor on the education pages of a national newspaper who had accepted a couple of articles from me on the subject of getting into medical school in the previous 12 months. She suggested that I should write a book after phoning me for advice on how to answer a reader's question about applying to university to study medicine. The

1

Introduction

paper's advice columnist, an ex Chief Inspector of Schools, was stuck for an answer on a particular query and so was she. I was able to answer her immediately. On that day it struck home that during my daughters' application cycle I had done a lot of very valuable and detailed research, and this book is an opportunity to share it.

In this book I talk about what we did and what we know from our experiences so other types of courses, such as graduate entry, foundation or access courses are not discussed. Neither is UKCAT, which was introduced the year after my two applied (phew), although the principles would be the same as for the exams they did take (which are discussed later). My daughters were both successful in securing offers on a standard undergraduate course. Martha received one offer and Molly got two. This probably doesn't sound like much to celebrate and, for straight A-grade students applying for any other subject but medicine, it wouldn't be. Six applications mostly translates into four, five or even six offers when you are predicted all A grades at A2. If you are applying to study medicine you are limited to a maximum of four medical school choices in the first place and from those most applicants are grateful to get just one offer.

Medical school offers are extremely difficult to acquire, one is all you need, two is a bonus and anything else the equivalent of a tickertape parade of acceptances. Getting a single medical school place, wherever it is in the UK, is a HUGE challenge even for the brightest students but one place is all they need.

There are no guarantees and I don't give any in this book. What I can provide is the certainty that you will have taken every step to support your son or daughter's application to medical school; if they are still unsuccessful you won't later be racked with self-recrimination and regret.

Introduction

WHO WANTS TO BE A DOCTOR ?

Let's be honest here. If your teenage son or daughter declares that they'd like to be a doctor, the news will most probably make you happy and proud. Medicine is a secure, respectable and honourable profession.

But. There's always a but. This is not Casualty, ER or Grey's Anatomy. This is your son or daughter's life under discussion. Remember, no matter how thrilled you are that they have chosen medicine, you must help them without carrying them along in the wake of your excitement. They have to lead the way regardless of how thrilling you think it will be to have a doctor in the family.

If you take over, then your son or daughter becomes enmeshed in this challenging process mostly to please you. What will they say at interview when they are asked that all important question 'Why medicine?' If they were honest some would have to answer 'because my mum or dad really wants me to be a doctor'.

Strike a balance. Acknowledge the enormity of what your son or daughter is undertaking and then strip away any tendencies you have to declare how very proud you are about the prospect of having a doctor in the family. Save it for six years time when they have qualified, when you can then pop with pride. Parental pressure and parental pride can be

5

indistinguishable to an overworked, overwrought and overtired sixth former in the middle of the medical school application process. Be useful without being emotional. You're helping them follow their dream, NOT yours.

No teenager wanders into a place at medical school. Getting a place to study medicine at university requires more forward thinking and precision planning than any other career choice. Throw top-notch grades and a huge capacity for hard work into that mix and you certainly have a teenager to be proud of. However, you won't be there when they are interviewed and you won't be there when they are beneath the landslide of textbooks and lecture notes for their termly exams. Your pride and excitement might help to propel them onto the course but it won't help them to stay on it unless they're doing it for themselves.

Your teenager needs appropriate help and support to achieve a place at medical school, what they don't need is you trying to convince them that being a medic is what they want. They have to get to first base by themselves; be sure you let them.

So, before we get to the nitty-gritty, are you able to answer the central question in this entire process truthfully? Don't hurl yourself into helping your son or daughter apply for medical school without an honest answer..... WHO WANTS THE PLACE? If it's you and not your child - forget it. You can't do it or buy it for them.

WORK EXPERIENCE AND SHADOWING

No work experience or shadowing – no chance. That's how important these are to your son or daughter's application.

Getting some suitable experience is the problem. We started in what seemed to us the most obvious place, our long time family doctor's surgery. The conversation went as follows. Molly asked, "My sister and I are applying to university to study medicine and hoped there might be opportunities for work experience in the practice, please?" Our GP replied, "Oh no. That would be for family and friends only". Like so many other aspects of applying to study medicine the entire process is so much easier if you have a medical connection. We didn't, so it was Plan B for my girls.

Molly and Martha wrote over 30 letters to private and NHS hospitals, care homes, children's homes and hospices offering themselves for work experience and drew a blank with all of them. The replies stated either that any placements they had were filled months before, that they didn't accept students for legal reasons or to protect patient confidentiality. Most did not bother to reply to their letters.

Running out of options they exploited a twice-removed contact with a Consultant. Their aunt had been treated as a private patient two years earlier by

7

a kindly surgeon and Molly and Martha begged her to approach this doctor on their behalf and plead for any work experience opportunity. That doctor's practice was very small so she was unable to help but did put the girls in contact with a colleague. He is a cardiac surgeon and invited Molly and Martha to his NHS unit in a leading London hospital where they were able to observe surgical and non surgical care over a three day period during the summer holiday that bridged Years 11 and 12.

The girls would have stretched those three days to three weeks, they enjoyed their time in the cardiac unit so much. The team allowed Molly and Martha to shadow them, observe them breaking bad news to a patient's family, witness a procedure to draw excess fluid from around a patient's heart and explained how the life support systems operated.

Molly and Martha saw close up the pressure that junior doctors experience from patients and their families and even from their own Consultant but remained undeterred. Their time at the hospital made the girls even more certain that a career in medicine is the right one for them.

Most university selectors would not consider one short 'shadowing' placement to be adequate preparation for life as a medical student so for Molly and Martha the hunt for a longer work experience placement continued. Bearing in mind that medical school applications must be submitted by early October of Year 13, work experience will need to have been completed or be well under way by this point in time. We learnt the hard way that it is smart to be quick off the mark and make contact with likely opportunities in Year 11. That way, your son or daughter will beat the rush and have time to invent and resort to plans X Y and Z if finding a placement proves difficult.

Our second bout of work experience was a weekly session at a cancer hospice where we volunteered as meal hostesses. Yes. I said we. I went too. When I mentioned this in a Sunday Times article I was derided on their letters page and medical school chat forums. My crime was that mummy muscled in on their work experience. I want to explain.

The only hospice interested in their request to volunteer was the one where my mum, their nan, had died. It was a long drive from the girls' school and they could only get there on time if I picked them up after school and drove them there.

On their first visit I brought a book and sat in my car reading and snoozing as I waited for them for two and a half hours. When they had finished they told me how busy it was at mealtimes and it struck me as daft that I would sit doing nothing in particular instead of putting on a pinny and helping out, too. So that's what I did every week thereafter. My help was given for the benefit of the hospice and the patients. Molly and Martha have since gone off on their gap years and on to university and I still go to help out at the hospice whenever I can. What a villain.

Volunteering at the hospice became one of the highlights of our week. We too had lost a loved one there and empathised strongly with the suffering of the patients and their families. Yet our time there was consoling and healing and, weird as this must sound, we just had so much fun. We were trolley dollies for drinks, meals and jelly fruit and ice cream (all three of us had our own speciality) and washer uppers. Working there gave the girls a valuable insight into how NHS resources are used and abused, and the pressures that medical teams have to endure. The girls met some very memorable people at the hospice and learnt to be patient and gracious, even with those who were *very* impatient with them.

Work experience is essential; it must feature on your son or daughter's personal statement. It will be discussed if they are called to interview so in that sense can be viewed as a means to an end. But it is so much more than that, it's an opportunity for your son or daughter to mature into medicine and test their commitment to a career as a doctor. They will experience working in a team and learn speaking and listening skills in a setting with real patients and their families.

Be quick off the mark organising work experience opportunities. The ideal is two contrasting placements, one where your son or daughter can observe patients being treated and another where they can at some level be involved in patient care.

Contact any local hospitals, GP surgeries, care homes, day centres or nurseries that are within travelling distance. Get your son or daughter to ask the entire extended family and friends old and new whether they have any medical contacts. Encourage them to 'think outside the box', talk to teachers at school, the local pharmacist, lollipop lady, rabbi, priest or your denominational equivalent to find a placement in a caring setting. Arranging useful work experience is a test of their resourcefulness, one which they must not fail.

Once the day dawns and they're actually off to do their work experience, recommend they take a notepad and keep a diary of events. It is likely to be some months before they write about the placement in their personal statement and even longer before they are (hopefully) interviewed and expected to discuss what they did, what they saw and, most importantly, what they learned.

My son has a friend who is currently in his fourth year studying medicine. He recounted his hospital work experience placement seven years ago. He arrived bright and early at the Human Resources Division of the hospital that had kindly organised his sessions. A member of the administrative team greeted him, handed him a white coat, a stethoscope and a name badge stating Junior Doctor and waved him off towards the wards with the instruction "Make yourself at home." Happily for the patients they didn't give him a syringe, a scalpel or a prescription pad. This 'relaxed' approach to work experience no longer exists, it is hard to come by and your son or daughter will have to meet high professional standards during their placement.

To recap, in medical school terms work experience is about your son or daughter testing their interest in medicine by spending time with vulnerable people. It is an unrivalled opportunity for your son and daughter to communicate with 'patients',

Work experience and shadowing

although the frail, elderly or children can fit into that category. It's about contributing in a care setting.

Work experience is not the same as shadowing. Shadowing is when prospective medics get an opportunity to watch the great and the good at work in a medical setting. Although it is valuable to have had both work experience and shadowing to discuss and contrast in your personal statement and at interview, it's the work experience, hopefully sustained over a significant period of time, which will boost the calibre of your son or daughter's application.

GRADES

The raw material for an undergraduate medical student is a young person with a string of A* and A grades at GCSE in intellectually demanding subjects, AABb at AS and AABb at A2, although AAAa is the gold standard. These glittering grades are your starting blocks but don't guarantee you a single offer. It really is that tough. With so many applicants for each place medical schools simply don't need to be flexible about grades.

The only reason universities may exercise some discretion about grades achieved/predicted would be extenuating circumstances. However, remember that admissions officers are tough, time-poor people who don't want to hear about how the death of your favourite goldfish or athlete's foot adversely affected your exam performance. To be taken seriously extenuating circumstances have got to be in the category of life altering trauma and you will need to be able to document any claims you make *and* have them supported by your school and your doctor. Inventing extenuating circumstances to try to skirt grade requirements is not an option.

I can already hear a chorus staring up, "I know someone at my son's second cousin's friend's school with a GNVQ in Tourism who got offered a place last year to study medicine at Cambridge". Well, maybe they did but more likely they didn't and anyhow you shouldn't be wasting time worrying about what

13

grades somebody else got, how they got them and where they got accepted – focus on what's happening under your own roof. Make sure your son and daughter know that having the grades is an essential first step that will entitle them to apply.

I am constantly amazed that potential applicants often don't bother to research grade boundaries and subject preferences of individual medical schools. Unless your son or daughter has checked for the year in which they are applying at each of their chosen universities, then they are essentially tossing their application into the wind.

It starts with GCSE results. Check the websites of the universities that offer medical degrees. Some are open and transparent and declare that they have a policy of using the number of A and A* grades as an element of their selection process when deciding who gets an interview. Others don't declare that they use GCSE grades as a filter and then swiftly reject applicants who don't meet their *unpublished* quota of A and A* grades.

For the record, I'm in favour of visible and declared grade thresholds. Yes, they are a tough and one-dimensional way of measuring ability and potential but they are also transparent. Grade boundaries make at least one strand of the medical school application system clear and, whilst it may dash the hopes of those who have lower grades and exclude them from applying, that's better and kinder than dragging out the process and fanning false hope. Making a good application to medical school is the sum of several years of effort and to be rejected outright because you can't compete with the exam grades that other candidates hold is valuable time wasted. It can also spoil your future chances, because at certain universities re-applicants are not welcome – so BEWARE.

Timing is all, if your son or daughter can overwhelm weakish GCSE grades with some stunning AS and A2 grades their application will get a boost. That could mean waiting another academic year to apply but the alternative is a graduate entry medical course after a first degree. Taking a productive gap year and then applying for medicine as a first degree can be a lot less stressful and expensive than alternative entry routes and postgraduate qualification.

I printed off the postgraduate application statistics from medschoolsonline.co.uk to show my daughters that you can't breeze into medical school even when you have a really good first degree. They were shocked by the gruesome statistics. Last year there were 62.5 applicants per place for postgraduate medicine at Kings College, London, for example. The prospect of another and tougher scrum for a postgraduate medical school place at 21 motivated them to work even harder to secure their A2 based offers. Yes this meant extra grocery shopping for me, it seemed they couldn't revise without eating, but they're worth their weight in biscuits.

Double check and cross-reference your son or daughter's predicted grades with the stated academic criteria for entrance to individual medical schools – don't assume they are all the same; they're not. Read these guidelines as the bare minimum expectation. In the year that my daughters applied our anecdotal evidence was that all the applicants who got interviewed were those who *exceeded* the stated grade requirements. In their school year the student who applied to medical schools with the weakest grades had rejections from all four universities within *three* weeks of submitting her form.

One of my daughters had 6 A* and 5 A grades at GCSE, 4 high B grades at AS and predictions of 4 A grades at A2. She liked Peninsula Medical School and selected it as one of her four precious UCAS choices. Molly telephoned the admissions office before submitting her application to check they would consider her and was answered with the good news that she actually exceeded their minimum academic requirements. Two months later she was bitterly disappointed to learn that she had been rejected without interview. When she requested feedback the reason given for her rejection was that she had B grades at AS and that they were only calling candidates to interview if they had A grades at AS. It felt to her like they had changed their selection criteria in the middle of the application cycle and that she had essentially chucked one of her four precious choices into the bin. She contacted the admissions department at Peninsula for more information and a member of staff clarified the situation for her by explaining that only 'local' candidates with B grades at AS were being considered for interview. "Clear as mud" said a sad Molly when she realised she'd blown one of her four choices. Interestingly she got her only interview and subsequent offer from a university who had a higher stated grade threshold than Peninsula.

Universities overwhelmed with applications have to take drastic steps to cull the number of candidates invited for interview but I implore medical schools to please, please, please give prospective students the full facts about entry requirements and all other admissions criteria so that they can be fully understood prior to making crucial choices about where to apply. Then, at least for the duration of that application cycle, stick to them.

It's depressing to have to write this but it's a trust no-one scenario. Read and re-read university prospectuses about entrance requirements. Go to the Open Days and have bat ears to hear what's being said and sometimes more importantly understand what's NOT being said. My daughters and their friends are very trusting and delightfully unspoilt by cynicism. It's been quite sad to observe them coming to terms with one of the harsh realities of life; people and organisations don't always say what they mean and mean what they say.

Prospective medics only get four choices on their UCAS form; wasting one on an application and later discovering they never had a realistic prospect of being selected for interview is hugely frustrating. Open Days are a great way to gather anecdotal information. Try to speak directly to Admissions Tutors. Better still, find a current student who will almost certainly be able to give 'off the record' insights into what the present cohort of students have in the way of grades. It's a shifting scene so be sure to speak to a student from the newest intake, they'll have the inside track information. Molly and Martha asked questions including which subject combinations does the university prefer? What happens if you slip a grade on results day - could you still be accepted and do they have a waiting list? Knowledgeable and up to date answers from current students made my girls feel more confident that their choices were good and realistic ones.

Getting a place at a UK medical school is a bun-fight. The difficulty in acquiring a place at medical school is not down to the difficulty of the course but the crush of applicants trying to secure offers each year. That's why your Doctor- to-be needs to view grades; GCSE, AS and A2 as essential rungs on the ladder. Without the grades they are going nowhere.

So to recap, get them to bust a gut revising because nearly there, as in 'I missed a grade by only three marks', sadly won't do. It will get your son or daughter a lot of good quality and very sincere sympathy but it won't get them a place at medical school. Offers are set in stone and if they don't get AAB their dream is almost certainly over for an undergraduate place. Flexibility on grades is rarer than rocking horse poop and without the grades for medical school, they can be a nurse, a health care worker, a ward clerk or numerous other valuable members of the care team. But they can't be a doctor.

GRADES IN WHAT SUBJECTS?

For medicine it's the killer combo – grades and subjects. Your offspring will be too young to remember Maureen Lipman in the BT ads in the 1980's, perhaps you do? In my twenties I thought it was silly but now, two decades later, the proud and loving gran putting a positive spin on bad exam result news seems so sad and sweet. Maureen Lipman played Beattie, the granny who had baked a celebratory cake in anticipation of her grandson's O Level results. Beattie was sitting down at the kitchen table placing the finishing touch, a handmade icing scroll, on top of the cake when her grandson telephoned. It was not good news – he had only passed in two subjects, pottery and sociology. Upbeat Beattie went into proud grandmother mode and declared that an O Level in pottery was fantastic because 'people will always need plates' and as for the sociology?' She declared 'if you've got an 'ology' you're a scientist!' Some 'ologies' are valuable medical school currency, others have little or no value at all.

For medical school biology good, sociology bad. Psychology? Don't know; the jury is still out. Drama, PE, Media and Art are also, generally speaking, not traditional medical schools' favourite A Level subjects. At the start of Year 12 both Molly and Martha were keen to take PE as their fourth AS subject and every medical school they contacted before making their application to enquire about its value on a medical school application said yes, they would accept it. Nonetheless we all remained nervous about them choosing PE, fearing it would be perceived as an easy option and not carry enough academic weight in the selection process when compared with another candidate's Physics or History or Economics. For this reason the girls decided to go for more traditional subjects, Mathematics and Latin respectively.

I know that exam boards and diligent students taking these subjects will argue vehemently against our thoughts on right and wrong subjects and there will be no hard evidence trail to support what we have said. However, I stick by the assertion that if you are an able student with the right GCSE grades from a good school the expectation will be that you compete for a place at medical school with four traditional and academically rigorous AS subjects. My daughters didn't choose PE, and went for combinations of Biology, Chemistry, Mathematics and Latin at AS and A2. Emerging 2 years later with one offer and two offers respectively Martha and Molly don't have any regrets about not choosing PE. In fact they are both convinced that if they had they would have been reapplying this year and not enjoying their planned gap year activities.

Universities have individual quirks, some favour candidates with at least one humanities subject amongst their AS choices and are good enough to say so in their prospectus or during their open days. Other universities still lean towards the traditional sciences and mathematics combination. Many don't particularly value the Maths/Further Maths double act believing there is too much repetition in their syllabuses.

Our combined opinion on A Level subject choices is: don't be kooky and gamble your chances of getting an offer first time around. If you want to show the selectors your flair for fashion, sculpture or body art do that as an extra curricular activity and refer to it in your personal statement, or hang a crystal off the end of your nose for Freshers' Week. Why gamble so early with your life choice career? Play safe with your subject choices because it's one less thing to worry about or regret later. There are many reasons why a good candidate may be rejected from medical school, don't make your AS and A2 subject choices one of them. That's suicide by subject.

Grades in what subjects?

TEACHER KNOWS BEST?

Subject teachers can often hold the key to the outcome of a sixth former's medical school application. Some may have twenty years teaching experience behind them, others may have qualified only months before your son or daughter approaches them for help. They can be responsible for assessing and declaring a student's predicted grades, commenting on the all-important personal statement and have input in the preparation of your son or daughter's reference.

What teachers are predicting on the UCAS form can be a big stumbling block. Some students are unsure about what their teachers will declare as their predicted grades because school policy varies so much. Some have a clear and stated policy about predictions; others are woolly on the topic. In my daughters' case their school took the line that it would only ever predict one grade above achieved AS grades. That was their non-negotiable policy. In other schools it can be left to the discretion of individual teachers and their professional judgement and some are prepared to be more lenient than others. I think this is one of many examples of (sorry about the cliché) the uneven playing ground in medical school applications.

There are many students who can recover AS grades with resits and who will go on to get AAB or AAA at A2, but teachers vary between wildly over-confident

23

and depressingly conservative when predicting grades on UCAS. A school reticent to declare the required grades can effectively block an application. Conversely schools that dispense gung-ho A2 predictions means that students without a realistic chance of getting the grades can make their way into the system and may get offers that they are unlikely to meet. These places could have gone to a student with better potential. Universities can now access AS module results and this may moderate the effects of school-generated inconsistencies in the application process.

To eliminate any doubt about predicted grades I encouraged my daughters to visit each subject teacher in turn in the first few days of the Yr 13 Autumn term armed with a sheet of paper. The girls then asked their teachers to write down what their predicted grades would be. This simple exercise had two useful functions, it boosted my daughters' confidence levels early in the application process because their teachers confirmed that they believed that AAA was achievable for them both, and it gave the teachers a chance to see Molly and Martha's focus and determination. Sixth form teachers typically predict grades for 100 plus pupils; it is important for your son or daughter to make it personal and impress on their teachers how committed they are to getting into medical school.

Getting some of their overworked, underpaid and occasionally downright disinterested teachers to commit to Molly and Martha's grade predictions in a face-to-face meeting was a good and positive start to their application process. Of course some teachers are so busy and distracted that you could sit in

24

front of them naked from the waist up twirling your gold lame nipple tassels and they still wouldn't look up from their mark books.

Even the best teachers can make genuine mistakes. I have heard horror stories of keyboard slip-ups, which end up with the wrong grades being entered on UCAS forms. Pupils and parents can't check at the time what the school has submitted and errors only become obvious much later in the application cycle when they are very difficult to rectify. Essentially you are at the teacher's mercy so try to make it personal by getting your son and daughter to explain what they need and why. Then when you are parked in front of the teachers at parents evening...... tell them all over again. Bore them into submission if you must. You don't want your child's ambitions to founder on a teacher saying "Oh, but I didn't realise little Jonny wanted to be a Doctor. I would have offered extra tuition and/or shown him some sample personal statements and/or offered interview training at lunchtime and/or introduced him to my first cousin Professor Getintomedschool. If *only* I'd known!"

No matter how spectacularly disinterested their subject teachers may be by the time they get to the end of AS year, Miss Dozeonthejob and her colleagues are all you have to work with. Have you heard the phrase 'you catch more flies with honey?' If not, commit it to memory and apply it. Complaints and rebukes will probably not get your son or daughter the predictions and references they need. You could have a gentle word with the Head of Sixth Form or even the Head Teacher if you feel that the subject teachers are so far tuned out to your child's application that they could choke it to death with their indifference. But be very careful because sour school staff can make life very difficult if they choose. Like I said earlier NO ONE will care as much about your child's future plans as you do, so take what you need from the school but be self-reliant, too. Check that what needs to be done has been done and that it happened on time, too.

I realise my comments about teachers sound like I'm bashing them. I'm not at all. My own husband has been a teacher for over 25 years and is one of the many good guys in the profession, completely dedicated to his job and his students. After all these years he is still excited by the positive influence he can have over so many lovely young people, but he believes that some elements of Sixth Form work should be dealt with only by specialists. There are countless teaching professionals like him who will genuinely care about your child's well being and their future, and that's great. But caring isn't enough. Nursery schools do that. Sixth Forms need to propel their students upwards and onwards.

 The best Sixth Forms have key staff who are experts in meeting the challenges of securing offers from medical school, Oxbridge and Russell Group universities. Good tutors know how to match student and university expectations. They have a set of skills to help students make expert applications and a sense of urgency about the process. Their influence can manoeuvre an application into the front line. Hooray for them and what they can achieve but, sadly, very few sixth formers have access to such gold standard support.

The reality is that overstretched and under-resourced schools have inexperienced and/or disinterested staff tinkering with personal statements and writing banal references that in medical school terms could sabotage the outcome of an application.

Some schools have several applicants for medicine each year and others one every few years. Some candidates I have spoken to say they are the first from their school EVER to apply to medical school and fear they will be disadvantaged for this reason. Practice doesn't always make perfect. My daughters' school had a good and useful programme up and running to support Oxbridge applicants, managing to get four or five offers each year and yet there was a big squelchy nothing for their annual four or five prospective medics; they are left to their own devices year after year.

Sometimes if your child is a lone or first time applicant this can be a good thing, galvanising the school into supportive and proactive mode. Then, of course, there are the experts - gold standard schools and colleges that have the entire process covered. They are few and far between but they do exist and give their candidates a priceless head start in terms of confidence and know-how. I know of a local Sixth Form College that rounds up their prospective medics early in Year 12, takes them on group work experience sessions at the local hospital, has guest speakers to address current medical issues twice each term and organises individual and group interview practice sessions. This type of preparation is modelled on what has typically been offered in good independent schools and fosters a strong 'can do' attitude amongst their students.

I believe that Medical Schools should have outreach programmes for Sixth Form Colleges, including staff as well as the students. A 'how to' session about maximising the impact of a reference and personal statements would be a great starting point. Teachers need support and guidance too and, by and large, are grateful when they get it.

THE REFERENCE

Here's the rub with the reference. It's got to be confidential before dispatch, so this mystery document that has so much impact on the strength of an application is sent unseen by the candidate. That's bearable and fair if you are certain that the person who wrote it knew how best to structure it and what to include. Don't assume that they do. Get involved and research what's needed on their behalf. If they turn out to be a medical school reference writing expert and your input isn't needed what's the worst they can call you and your son or daughter? Tenacious, and that's good.

I tried to get some clear direction by emailing the Admissions Officers at some of my daughters chosen universities claiming that my child was home educated and requesting guidance on what should be addressed in the academic reference. What came back was very useful; universities that replied wanted a detailed academic profile along with comments about school based achievements and extra curricular interests. They expected the student would have experience in caring or mentoring roles in and out of school. The importance of strong communication skills, both speaking *and* listening was flagged, as was the student's capacity to work independently and as part of a team. They asked for evidence of these attributes. Details and supporting documentation for any extenuating circumstances that impacted on

The Reference

the candidate's performance was requested too. One university stressed that it expected teachers to state the obvious - that the candidate was enthusiastic and hardworking. All expected the reference writer to strongly or highly commend the candidate's character and disposition and overall suitability for a career in medicine.

When we read the university pointers, the girls and I made a list of all their relevant individual personal achievements and cross-matched them to the guidelines. We were able to tailor their skills and experiences to the various reference categories and we emphasised the essential points using highlighter pens to catch their tutor's eye. This research had the potential to make their references more detailed and targeted, with the bonus effect of making their teachers' task easier. In the Sunday Times Article these actions were briefly described and our critics pounced, wailing that we had cheated by writing our own references.

Molly and Martha were meticulous in listing each and every skill, attainment, volunteering opportunity and paid and unpaid work over a four year period. They included some earlier achievements when they were especially pertinent, together with positive comments that had been made by teachers, trainers, tutors and employers. Combining information we had sourced on the Internet, at Open Days and in prospectuses we included words and phrases that we considered would be highly desirable in a personal reference.

Everything we wrote was 100% true and verifiable. We packaged information for the teachers so it was clear and accurate and easy for them to use. We had no influence over whether they opted to use it or not but it is highly likely that they did – mostly because it was right there. One teacher said that she thought the reference 'pro forma' initiative showed what a good doctor Martha would make and how it had illustrated her dedication and attention to detail.

I've reproduced the list which we sent to their teachers in an appendix at the end of this book so that you can, if you choose, adapt it to your child's skills and attainments. The words and phrases that are desirable on a personal reference are general but you should also read the prospectuses of your chosen medical schools carefully and include any others that you believe might be particularly apt.

Most teachers these days use computer generated lists of words and phrases to describe their pupil's level of attainment when writing end of year reports so, by providing them with a personalised list like the one I'm describing, this reference prompt is just another useful sixth form resource. Thankyouverymuch should be the response of any reasonable teacher but remember the list must be fact based – teachers and Admissions Officers generally possess well-honed bull****ometers.

The Reference

PERSONAL STATEMENTS AKA THE CLINCHER

The personal statement is, in most cases, what gets your son or daughter called for interview. In the vast majority of UK medical schools no interview means no offer means no Doctor. The personal statement had better be brilliant, and more, and the rest, in 47 lines of 12 point type and a maximum of 4,000 characters. Explain to your son or daughter that it is not a requirement that it should be exactly 4,000 characters long. Perhaps that sounds blindingly obvious but anxiety can often cancel out common sense.

Whether it's your son or daughter, or in my case daughters, writing a personal statement for medical school my practical advice to you is to invest in some body armour or leave home for a few weeks. The mood that prevailed at personal statement time in our house was severe premenstrual tension crossed with high grade teenage angst crossed with acute toothache.

My girls went bonkers. For seventeen years they had co-existed as incredibly close and peaceful twin sisters, arguments were very rare. But when it came to their personal statements they became ultra moody, secretive and highly suspicious of one other and anyone else that got to read the early drafts.

These drafts were handled like top secret, classified documents. At the height of personal statement

33

fever I think they would have eaten the sheet of A4 with the personal statement printed on it before allowing anyone else to read it if they weren't in the right frame of mind for constructive criticism.

Theirs was the only definition of constructive criticism that counted. I was barricaded out of their rooms and reduced to going through waste paper bins to learn what was in the first drafts of their personal statements. No comment was permitted. Zero tolerance. Any early attempt to offer my opinion was countered by piercing shrieks and a lunge at the fridge for some more chocolate.

Seeing that the task was creating so much stress for them I did try to help on several occasions and would start a conversation in a low, calm voice with 'Molly/Martha, hello....' And whichever daughter I was 'attacking' (that's how they perceived it) would upend the chair she was sitting on and flounce out of the room before slamming the door so hard it made my teeth fillings rattle. The two things that they said most frequently at personal statement time were 'I can't do this!' and 'It's bullshit!' accompanied by the sound of tearing paper. They read and re-read the statements aloud, pecked at the punctuation until perfect and on a couple of rare occasions actually declared themselves happy with it before they went to bed. Only to wake up a 3am, get up, delete it and start all over again.

Writing a personal statement can induce despair. It's especially perverse that many potential doctors whose natural inclinations are towards the sciences aren't always fluent in expressive prose. Yet so much relies on their ability to write a sincere and compelling personal statement describing why they have what it takes to train and qualify as a doctor. It's an agonising challenge for many prospective medics; a painful birthing experience that will hopefully culminate in a little bundle of paper that will make them happy and proud for the rest of their lives.

Persuade your son or daughter to take a rational overview of what the personal statement is and what its purpose is. That might help them take a cooler approach to this exercise. The personal statement isn't an implement of torture, it's the first test of their communication skills in the medical recruitment process. They have to rise to the challenge of providing specific information within a given word limit. It's their chance to make a controlled first impression and one which, unlike an interview, can't be dominated by nerves.

Last week I went to a Sixth Form Information Meeting at a local school. Even though my daughters are both safely into medical school I felt compelled to go because the Admissions Officer from a leading London medical school had accepted an invitation to address the students and their parents/carers. I was eager to hear her speak about the application process. It was fascinating to see an Admissions Officer in the flesh; I had imagined Cruella de Ville but got Maria from the Sound of Music. She sang, I mean spoke, about all aspects of applying to medical school including what makes a good personal statement starting with the don'ts. She had two favourites from the most recent batch of applications, one that started with the words 'I am boring', and another which included some drawings of the prospective candidate coping in various medical emergency situations. Neither applicant got to the interview stage. There's a surprise.

She stressed that a personal statement should convince selectors that your son or daughter have the potential to be a good doctor, will complete the course and actually use the qualification they get. In other words - are they deserving of the £250,000 plus it will cost to train them? She gave clear pointers about the value of a good personal statement and referred prospective medics to the good advice about content which can be found in books and on the Internet.

What my girls found most challenging was how to give this A4 sheet of facts and figures *heart*. Molly and Martha both struggled with expressing the answer to the most obvious and only compulsory element in their personal statements - Why do I want to be a Doctor? You may think it would be ridiculously easy to answer that question, particularly when they spent the last two years planning their applications and even longer than that making medicine their career choice. But they agonised about how their answer to this question would be scrutinised and judged and tied themselves up in convoluted knots trying to be arresting and original in order to capture the attention of the selectors.

In the end, with some persuasion from me, they settled for sincerity over being scintillating at the beginning of their personal statements and the rest seemed to flow naturally from that. The 'why do you want to be a doctor?' question is so central to making a convincing application that your son or daughter needs to be able to answer this on paper and to articulate it without struggling.

An excellent way to approach this declaration is by hooking your initial desire to be a doctor to a 'moment'. But definitely not the plagiarised 'setting fire to pyjamas with a chemistry kit' moment which **233** applicants claimed as their own in last year's admissions cycle! Other personal statement openers that gave selectors déjà vu included 370 applicants who declared themselves 'fascinated by the human body' and too many to be true who had a 100 year old granddad who had inspired them to study medicine.

Having an inner certainty about practising medicine is lovely and admirable but your son or daughter has to translate that into an **outer** certainty by being able to write about their inclinations and convictions. To carry any value their ideas have to be articulated.

I've always wanted to be a writer. That was simply understood in my household where from the age of seven years old I was usually to be found in the corner of the settee with my nose deep into an Enid Blyton book, or scribbling into a notepad.

When I was ickle twice a year we would get a visit from our formidable Aunt Winifred. She was fed, watered and feted, not least because she gave away £5 notes to her favourite nephews and nieces as she headed for home. I was around 9 years old when she boomed in my direction 'And what is it *you* want to be when you grow up?' Without hesitation and clutching my notepad to my heart as evidence I answered 'A writer Aunt Winifred'. She arranged her features into a benign smile during a silence deep enough to fall into and be lost forever. Light years later she spoke again in a low voice, 'Why?' That's an easy question I thought to myself as I replied 'I don't really know, I just know that I do, Aunt Winfred'.

I didn't get a fiver from her that day or ever again. My credibility was shattered. In her eyes I was just dreaming. She spat back 'Hah! Did the fairies tell you?' and remembering those words and her snort of laughter has hurt me every day since.

My inner conviction that I wanted to be a writer has, happily for me, turned into a body of published work. It's not that easy if you want to study medicine. Claiming that you know that's what you want to do is only the start. Having an inner certainty that you want to be Doctor means that you will have a lot of people to convince along the way. You need to test and confirm your inner drive with work experience and study so that when the admissions officers read your application your desire has been tested and your skills proven.

Your teenager wants to be a doctor. Why? Ask them to tell you. If they can't write and speak fluently about their reasons for wanting to study medicine or look you in the eye and describe them then they are not ready to apply – they are in trouble. I can't stress it enough; they must know the reasons, be able to write about the reasons and talk about the reasons. Have I laboured this point enough now? All the interviewees will have the right grades, a very good personal statement, excellent references and relevant work experiences. On the day it will be about which candidate expresses themselves the best. Who wants it most and why? If they can't be convincing on this central subject their application is in serious trouble.

My daughters had similar motivations for studying medicine, not that surprising as they are twin sisters. Molly and Martha are a good example of reasons for choosing medicine needing to be sincere more than they need to be original. My daughters were unfortunate and observed the treatment of a range of serious and some very rare family illnesses close up in their early years. Then a road accident left their beloved granddad severely brain damaged, he came to live with us and they became involved with his care; doctors and hospitals have loomed large in their young lives.

It fills me with regret that they had to witness so many traumas during their school years, but they have transformed what I thought were horrible and negative experiences into new beginnings. Their grandparents would be so proud of them if they were alive to see them start training as doctors. Molly and Martha left copies of the long awaited letters from UCAS confirming their places at medical school on their grandparents' grave. Your son or daughter will have their own sources of inspiration to write about, it's important that they find them and are able to share them because they're at the heart of their application.

Personal Statements

Next Molly and Martha wrote about their A Level subject choices, work experience, school responsibilities, paid work, hobbies and social life. Most important of all...they discussed what they had learnt from all their various experiences. The single biggest mistake I see when looking over personal statements for prospective medical students is a compulsion to make lists on the page.

Writing about your subjects, grades, volunteering or paid work is only interesting and revealing if you include personal insights after the facts. Even if your child has been lucky enough to observe a heart transplant, it will be of no more relevance on their personal statement than another candidate witnessing an ear wax removal if they don't state what they gained from the experience.

Molly, Martha and I devised an exercise where they had to qualify every significant event in their draft personal statement using the link .....'and from that I discovered *or* was shocked by *or* changed my beliefs *or* decided'..... finding it a very useful way of giving their personal statement depth. A lot of what they wrote when they did this simple exercise made its way into their final drafts.

Whilst suffering the in-house agonies of the personal statement season I saw that once again the girls' school fell short when it came to giving good advice and useful ideas. They were fine when it came to pointing out grammatical errors or spelling mistakes but gave no useful guidance at all on the suitability of the statement as a tool for admission to med school. Martha asked two staff members to read copies of her statement on the same day. Both were returned with single word comments. One said 'weak' and the other 'excellent'. This contradiction caused heightened drama at home as the she wailed over which of the comments to take on board.

What we all felt we needed at that time were a few examples of personal statements that had secured the writers an interview at a UK medical school. Trawling the Internet at that time the best I could come up with were examples of the American equivalent of a personal statement. These were more flowery than Kew Gardens. Some referred to angels, life's winding highways and love and worry boxes. Had the girls nicked any ideas from these samples for their personal statements a psychiatric referral would have been a more likely outcome than a medical school interview.

It was around this time that I had a conversation with a relative whose best friend's daughter was also applying to medical school. She was a pupil at a highly selective private school with a first class sixth form. Among the many resources available to Year 12 and 13 students was a bank of hundreds of personal statements from previous applicants to Oxbridge, Law and Medicine. Current sixth formers were able to read these statements and derive inspiration and encouragement from them. It struck me what a brilliant demystifying aide that would be when you are attempting to write a personal statement not just from cold but from below freezing: when you have never clapped eyes on such a document before. Or when no one in your school has applied to study medicine in the last decade and you don't have any friends or family members in the medical profession or knowledgeable teachers to steer you through the process.

Many students, like my daughters, who apply to university to read medicine will only ever see one personal statement, their own. I think this puts them at a huge disadvantage. That is why at the end of this chapter you will find my own daughters' personal statements along with several others.

I realise this may be considered controversial by those who believe that a personal statement should be precisely that, personal. However, when like my daughters you have absolutely no idea about how to pitch this document and other students you are competing with have easy access to a range of examples, it's simply unfair. I consider this to be one of many reasons why state school students make fewer applications to study medicine and are more likely to be rejected when they do.

I felt for my own daughters and anyone else year on year who struggles with the personal statement element of a medical school application. That's why I decided that the best way to help alleviate some personal statement stress was to publish a selection of personal statements with a declaration about how many interviews/offers/rejections each one generated.

This next bit is a severe warning like when a TV announcer says in a very grave tone after a woman in a gold lame cat suit sets fire to herself and back flips off a tall building, 'don't try this at home'. My warning is **Don't Plagiarise These Statements**. The spirit in which the writers shared their work and my decision to publish them is to encourage your child to unlock their own ideas and the ability to express them. These sample personal statements are intended to INSPIRE and boost confidence to a level where your son or daughter will be able to write a brilliant one of their own.

You'll glean from what follows that a good personal statement should tell the reader about who you are and why you have the potential to be a good doctor. Be sure to include some evidence that supports your entitlement to start and your commitment to finish an expensive course of training that will carry enormous responsibilities and trust.

My sincere thanks to all the generous personal statement donors who allowed us to read and reproduce their efforts here for the benefit of others. Names and personal details have been changed for obvious reasons of confidentiality.

Personal Statements

INTERVIEW READY?

After the girls pressed the SUBMIT button on their UCAS forms it felt as if the whole world fell silent. For what seemed like an AGE nothing happened. They checked UCAS track religiously, using advanced keyboards skills because mostly their eyes were squeezed tight shut as they opened the page. The big fear was they would see the word UNSUCCESSFUL next to one or...catastrophe...more of their choices. Each day they would return from school with news of interviews or offers for their school friends who were applying to study everything and anything but Medicine.

The earliest interview in their school cohort for medical school was in the last week of October and the latest we heard about was in June of the following year. Even their friends who had applied to Oxford and Cambridge had their interviews completed for all subjects well before Christmas. However, we welcomed in the New Year and the wait continued. Martha took to walking the dog before 7.00am so she could head off our postman at the top of the road and be sure of getting her post before going to school.

The girls' biggest worry was that the perceived delay meant they weren't going to be called for interview. They were convinced they were simply waiting to be rejected once they hadn't heard from any of their choices before Christmas. "Doomed, we're all doomed!" was their mantra because they assumed that the universities cherry pick their favourite candidates for the first interviews and then slot in the rest at a later date.

When I spoke with the Admissions Officer from a highly popular medical school she explained her school's approach to the 3,000 plus applications for 280 places, which they begin to process once the UCAS deadline has passed each year. Applications undergo initial checks to ensure they meet the minimum grade boundaries. Next they are dispersed to various members of the admissions panel who carry out a selection process with numerous elements including grades again, personal statement, reference and extenuating circumstances. This sifting is then crosschecked and candidates who have been selected for interview are notified. What I understood from her explanation is that, assuming minimum grade requirements are met, at the initial stages the selection process is multi-dimensional and you won't be interviewed or rejected on one element of the application alone.

She explained that the excruciating waiting period is solely due to the high number of applications they have to screen, and nothing to do with any internal ranking fiddledeedee, which she believes would be a waste of precious processing time. She stressed that every medical school has a different method of handling their applications, some are happy to reveal them and others keep them confidential for reasons unknown.

Finally it happened. Four months after they had submitted their applications the first interview letter arrived. After all the anticipation it felt like the invitation should have been written on a scroll parchment and delivered on a silver platter by a footman dressed in purple and gold. Actually it was a brown envelope that came second-class post.

Martha had been invited to interview and given 3 weeks notice of the date. The letter warned that the date and time offered was a one and only single chance, it would be virtually impossible to alter in any circumstances. For this reason I would strongly advise you to clear your son or daughter's diary of any important other appointments during November of the year they apply through to the following April, including any holidays, medical or dentistry consultations or immoveable work or work experience commitments.

As a regular visitor to the medical school related websites that have chat forums I'm always surprised when students ask again and again about what they should wear at interview. A suit, of course – what else? A medical school interview *is* a job interview so it is essential to look smart and show the selectors that the interview and its outcome are very, very important to you.

Hair and nails should be clean and conservative and any piercings and/or tattoos concealed. For one short period in their lives encourage your son or daughter to be middle of the road so that the selection panel don't have any prejudices to overcome or excuses to doubt the sincerity of their application or suitability for life as a Doctor.

Interview Ready?

Skirt or trouser suits were an alien concept to my daughters prior to their medical school interview, ditto smart leather shoes. There was a lot of walking and wailing around shopping centres before we tracked down the perfect suit in Tchibo of all places. The three of us had retired there for coffee and muffins, thoroughly defeated after a soul destroying, quarrelsome suit-shopping trip. And suddenly it rose up in front of us. On the sale rail and in direct view of where we had plonked ourselves down. A smart jacket and trousers in a flat pin striped cotton velvet that cost just £22. A gift? Divine intervention? Call that suit what you will but it stopped the three of us arguing and made both Molly and Martha look fantastic.

They both wore this to all three of their interviews and now call it their 'lucky' suit. It was fortunate they didn't have interviews at the same date or time. And no, it's not for hire because it's now in the wardrobe waiting for my youngest daughter to be called to interview or summoned to attend criminal court, whichever comes first.

Our interview training began at home. My sister, a Company Secretary for a huge international company, and I set up sessions on four consecutive Sunday afternoons in our kitchen. We arranged the dining table with three seats for the 'selectors' (her, me, their dad) on one side. The 'interviewee', Molly or Martha, was invited to sit on a single chair positioned six feet away on the other side of the table and prepare to be grilled.

These sessions had the flavour of the Mad Hatter's Tea Party about them. My husband would frequently forget which question he had asked in the first place and on one occasion nodded off mid interview because it was too soon after Sunday lunch for him to concentrate properly. Their Aunt frequently cried when one of the girls gave an especially good answer and would then wipe her eyes and blow her nose loudly as she declared 'She's doing so well, I'm very, very proud!' about whichever niece was in the hot seat. I admit it was all a bit Mickey Mouse. In a real interview situation there wouldn't be a tabby cat asleep on the table, nor would the panel and the interviewee be sharing salsa and crudités between questions.

For all of that those mock interviews at home were still very useful preparation. Even though these practices were done with kindly undertones we were scrutinising the girls and made some very frank observations about how they walked, talked and answered some of our questions. There was plenty of high volume opinion exchanges (shouting matches) and door slamming during the sessions. Often the panel (my husband, sister and I) would spend long periods sitting like ducks in a row behind the kitchen table waiting for one or another or sometimes both interviewees to get over a sulk and rejoin us. Molly and Martha laugh at their stroppiness now and admit that these homespun rehearsals *were* useful for helping them to verbalise ideas in front of an audience and to overcome their natural shyness. Molly thought the mock interviews taught her to 'speak like a human and not like a robot' and gave her 'confidence to cope with crazy adults'. I think I know what she means by that.

Interview Ready?

My sister who regularly interviews as part of her job and understands how nerve wracking the process can be encouraged the girls to go out onto the patio and perform star jumps prior to the practices. She firmly believed that these jumps would energise the girls and disperse some of their nervous energy. Molly and Martha reluctantly deferred to her greater knowledge and experience but took a while to locate a spot in the garden where the neighbours wouldn't be able to see them 'discharging their energy'. This explains why they could be found on Sunday afternoons during last October leaping up and down in bushes at the very back of the garden.

When it came to their real interviews Molly actually did her jumps in the ladies loo before she was called into the interview room but Martha said she was too tight with nerves and could hardly move at all, let alone perform star jumps. Instead she tried a few facial exercises to get her mouth moving so she would be able to speak when questioned. That was until she had the mad thought that there might be a hidden video camera in the waiting room catching her on film pulling faces and gurning. She decided to use her handbag to cover her face as she stretched and made eeeeh aaaaaah ooooh movements with her mouth. Martha's concentration was broken when the interviewer, who had approached unnoticed, tapped her on the shoulder and with a puzzled look gestured that she should follow her into the interview room.

Martha insisted I pay her before I was allowed to tell that story in this book. I hope you agree it was worth £20.

One of the most interesting aspects of interview training at home is how quickly the time passes. We set the kitchen timer for fifteen minutes and discovered that by the time the interviewee enters the room, says their hellos, sits down and answers an ice breaker question there is then only time for three or four further questions. We strongly encouraged Molly and Martha to approach each of the panel and greet them in turn with a firm handshake.

They recoiled from this idea at first and preferred to scuttle to their seat and wait, wide-eyed with terror, for their questions. So they could understand how panicked this made them look and what a poor first impression they made we asked each of them to sit in on the other's interview and even play at being a panel member for one another. After that they agreed that when they came into the room and made a dash for the chair they looked like road runner and agreed that, yes, they should calmly walk over and greet their interviewers before sitting down.

Sitting down sounds simple but even that wasn't straightforward. After trying out several positions we all agreed that sitting with their legs crossed over at the knee looked much too jaunty for interview, or worse still, too Sharon Stone. Knees bent and feet flat on the floor made their legs visibly tremble with nerves, so they opted for legs crossed at the ankle slightly to one side. Next came the arms arrangement. Hands clasped lightly and resting on their lap was voted the best deterrent to itching, twitching or twirling hair as they spoke. We also recommended that they make eye contact with each panel member in turn and ditch any tendency toward a mad stare directed at a spot on the wall behind us or, occasionally and scarily, at a single panel member. The final tip, which is a transferable skill that can also be applied during exams, interviews and childbirth, is to BREATHE. If you get too nervous and forget to breathe you'll end up speaking all high and squeaky – and who needs a Doctor with a Minnie Mouse voice?

Those fifteen minutes in the interview hot seat will be your son or daughter's chance to shine after almost two years preparation. They need to be able to convince the panel that they have a genuine and considered interest in medicine – that means familiarity with current issues around matters medical, some historical knowledge about developments in medicine and an opinion on likely future developments in the field. The questions that never go away are the ones about why they want to be a Doctor and why they want to train at that particular university. These are almost certain to pop up in one guise or another. In the appendix I've listed all the questions the girls were asked at interview, along with many others asked that year, and which therefore represent a good cross section of the type of questions your son or daughter are likely to get thrown at them.

I'm sure they have heard this advice numerous times before – they should be themselves - but their very nicest and most enthusiastic and least hysterical selves. The panel at a medical school interview haven't invited your son or daughter in to entertain them, so they need to be serious and resist any temptation to be jokey.

Molly said that she felt like rigor mortis had set in the first time she entered a medical interview room and that the desire to crack a joke was the furthest thing from her mind. What your son and daughter thinks may be a side splittingly funny remark could be the kiss of death for their application, so encourage them to be calm and do lots of interview practice with friends and family which should in some way prepare them for speaking in stressful situations without getting garrulous or panicked.

Some of our favourite daily reading while we waited (and waited) for the girls to receive a pile of interview invitations in the post were the medical school related websites and their interview sections. One of my favourite stories included the Oxford medical candidate who was shown a photograph of a dog on a laptop screen five minutes into her interview and then instructed by the interviewer to 'diagnose that'. Another memorable daft question came from an interviewer who pointed out of the window to a random building that had nothing to do with the university or medicine or anything at all and asked the very confuzzled interviewee 'What is that?' When I think of the practice, the professional training, the suit shopping and the star jumps that Molly and Martha put into their preparation I am so glad that neither of them were asked such dumb and time wasting questions as that. Molly and Martha laughed the loudest when they read the answer to the following question asked at interview 'What would you say to Martians to explain how the NHS has developed in the last 25 years?' The very nervous interviewee put his mouth into gear before his brain and answered 'Hello Martians'.

Interview Ready?

Molly got two interviews and two offers and Martha got one interview and one offer. They now say that without practice and professional help (more about that in the next chapter) they would have blown it and ended up with nothing. If your son or daughter believes they don't need any help preparing for their interview they are already in trouble. The competition is intense; other candidates are rehearsing, researching and shopping for outfits as you sit reading this. Without good and useful interview preparation your son or daughter may entertain the interview panel, they might even charm them but they will not convince them that they have what it takes to be one of tomorrow's doctors.

AFTER THE INTERVIEW

Both Molly and Martha were lucky and secured offers and, happily, they didn't have to wait too long for them. I heard screams of delight from Molly's room three days after her first interview when she discovered on UCAS track that she had a conditional offer. Both her second offer and Martha's single offer came through in less than a week. I have heard many prospective medical students saying that they can bear the wait as long as they finally get the offer.

Gina, a friend of my daughters decided in her own words 'to take a punt' at getting into medical school with borderline acceptable GCSE grades. She got one interview and was especially thrilled because this lone hope was at her first choice university. Post interview she heard she had been placed on their waitlist.

The medical school waitlist is purgatory. Depending on when you find out that your son or daughter is parked on a waitlist you won't enjoy your Christmas tree, your Easter egg and even your summer holiday. December through to August can all be spoilt by the nerve jangling suspense of not knowing if they have an offer or not. Gina finally got her answer in August, nine months after she submitted her application; after all that time it was a NO. It had taken nine months for her to fall off her wobbly waitlist perch and to make matters worse the university in question, her favourite, had a policy of not accepting re-applicants. Gina reluctantly started a Bio-Medical degree and to this day regrets rushing in and chucking her only opportunity of getting an undergraduate medical training place at her first choice university. Her lament is that she should have waited a year when her excellent AS and A2 grades combined with additional work experience may have buffed up and strengthened her application and maximised her chances.

Making a medical school application requires strategic planning, as many universities don't accept re-applicants. This means if your son or daughter has a strong preference about where they want to study they need to do all that they can to get it right first time.

Getting no offers is a rotten situation to be in, especially of your teenager worked hard for their grades and on their application. The only consolation I can offer is that they've chosen a tough application process and a demanding and highly competitive course; it's not a reflection on them. They must already be an alpha student to make a good medical school application and they have to be empathetic to be a good doctor. Experiencing and more importantly, coping with disappointment, is excellent preparation for life as a medic. Your son or daughter can demonstrate their genuine commitment to medicine by regrouping, reapplying and showing they can handle adversity.

GETTING THE EXPERTS IN

Yes, getting the paid experts in definitely maximises your child's chances of success when applying to medical school. Karl Marx would not approve of this proposition, and I can see his point. But you must decide what is it you want in the next 18 months – is it to reform the UK's education, health and tax systems? Or do you want to give your son and daughter the best shot at applying for medicine? If it's the latter then you have to shelve your social conscience if it's troubling you and spend your money. But wisely.

We were savaged by critics of my Sunday Times article who thought it was outrageous that I paid for an interview training course, BMAT tuition and a weekend at Medsim for my daughters. I was accused of 'buying' my girls a place to study medicine.

My spend on courses and tuition was no more than £600 on each daughter over two years. I have never paid school fees or tuition fees before so spread over the twelve years of their education, £600 was small fry. More importantly I think it was great value. They got to talk to doctors, they got to hear re-sit students discuss their experiences of applying and they got a good close up look and opportunity to listen to the competition. They got information and insights they simply could not have got from anywhere else at that time and I would happily have spent more if I could. Some of the services on offer came to our attention too late. Would we have paid for personal statement drafting or checking if we'd known it was out there? Perhaps. Our aim was to be successful and if I had felt that the girls were unhappy or unsure about any aspect of their application after we had done all that we could we might have sought further advice.

Maybe we wouldn't have needed paid support at all if their state school had been more assured about preparing medical school applicants, or if we had a close friend or relative in the medical profession who could reassure us that we had every base covered. Perhaps if we'd had the means to send the girls to a first class independent school that successfully processes numerous medical school applications each year and had fostered their confidence to the point where we were all three of us certain that no external help was needed then I needn't have got my cheque book out. The fact is that we were on our own, without medical or university connections, and wanted to make the best applications we could. Some of the courses proved more useful than others but none were a waste of their time and my money. Each one added something to their application and definitely boosted their confidence levels throughout the long and wearing admissions cycle.

Some families won't have the money to pay for these courses for their children, and that means they have to work harder and faster to get the maximum out of the free resources available. I've listed some of the sites and organisations that are useful for information gathering at the end of this chapter. I would stress again that at the forefront of every application is determination and personal commitment, neither of which are covered in any course designed to boost your son or daughter's chance of a place at medical school.

Students not attending any commercial courses should be at the front of the queue for the few state funded courses that are available. An excellent free way to gather information is by talking with prospective and current medical students. They can make contacts and read web logs on the many Internet sites that discuss medical school applications and share in these highly relevant personal experiences.

Molly and Martha went on Medlink's Medsim course. They had a whale of a weekend and declared it by far the most social of their preparation courses. It involved a two days and nights away at Nottingham University where they participated in various activities including useful CPR training and a mock emergency callout. For this crisis callout they were paged in the early hours of the morning and driven around campus in the back of an ambulance that travelled at top speed with sirens blaring. They declared it massive fun. Overall the course merited only one line in their personal statement but the anecdotal information they picked up about universities, grades, interviews and reapplying was priceless. They came home buzzing and doubly certain that medicine was the right career for them.

Next was their interview training course which they did with a company called Dr Prep Ltd. This was an intensive day of talks, training and finally a filmed mock interview. They got the CD to take home, review, and cringe over at their leisure. This was the real deal – the tutors and speakers were all working medics or specialists in their field and all the other candidates were equally focused on getting the most from the day's tuition. The girls felt they learnt a lot from the other delegates as well as the teaching staff.

Molly and Martha were given high quality and very pertinent post interview feedback that was both critical and constructive. Dr Prep's day was social but serious and hard work. Because this course was held in November, a month after applications had actually been submitted, every student present had real interviews looming and the stakes were very high. Both Molly and Martha now say that they thought this was the most targeted and useful of their paid for preparation and that they have retained a lot of the tips about coping with stress and answering interview questions well.

Molly who applied to two BMAT universities went on an exam preparation day organised by a company called Gradmed. This was of variable quality. She described their tuition as rushed and the marking of the test papers was not graded in the way the company had said it would be in their promotional material. When we pointed this out to the course organisers her work was remarked but her ranking in the group was never provided. This was one of the things that attracted us to the course in order to give Molly an idea of how she would perform against other similar candidates in an exam that was completely new to her.

Overall Molly felt the course had some positive elements, like doing the mock BMAT under timed conditions and some of the discussions about the wacky essay questions that had cropped up in past papers, for example 'Why Can't Plants Walk?'

There were eleven other students on this course with Molly and incredibly all of them had a close relative who was a Doctor. Although she said this made her feel a bit of an 'outsider,' she did acknowledge that was a brilliant opportunity to listen to their lunchtime chat which was peppered with insights about the hours worked and the stresses of being a medic. Molly observed that although the other students all said that their mum/dad/aunt/other relative complained frequently about the stresses of being a Doctor, it obviously hadn't deterred any of them from trying to get a place at medical school.

There are companies available who will offer help with personal statement drafting, university selection and finding relevant work experience. My advice would be to sample as much as you can afford but don't substitute paid for help with what your child should also be doing themselves: researching on the internet, making phone calls and acquiring all the inside track information needed for a good application. No paid organisation can revise for them, get the grades for them or sit in front of a tough interview panel and answer the hardball questions that will come their way. Help them as much as you can with and without your chequebook in hand before you start using outside agencies. Know enough about what services you are buying in to be able to judge their quality and value.

Getting the experts in

To the critics who responded in vitriolic terms to my
Sunday Times article decrying the fact that my
daughters had BMAT tuition and interview training
and declaring that they themselves managed to
secure a place in medical school without any help
from anybody, at all, ever, I say a sincere very well
done indeed to all of you. It's precisely because the
competition is peppered with brilliant guys and girls
of your ilk that most ordinary mortals urgently need
to seek some level of support with their application.
Will you be better Doctors for having no tuition or
interview training six years down the line? Who
gives a damn as long as all concerned are all doing a
good job?

IS THERE A DOCTOR IN *YOUR* HOUSE?

If your son or daughter has the grades and the burning ambition to study medicine I hope this book has demonstrated many positive ways that you can get involved with their application without ever crossing a line and trying to take it over.

You don't need any special skills to be an expert parent on the subject of getting into medical school. Mainly you need to be interested, curious and not easily discouraged. Have your reading glasses to hand and your common sense and chequebook at the ready.

Vital information about medical degree courses, admissions statistics and universities is out there for the taking and is completely free but be ready to acknowledge that there will be some things you can't tackle in-house. Choose expert help wisely and be sure about exactly what you are getting in exchange for your cash when you decide it is time to buy in some help.

Don't ever feel guilty about backing your son or daughter or believe that your actions and support are giving them any unfair advantages. There are more than twenty-five candidates competing for every place at some UK medical schools and you can be quite certain that the majority of them will have the grades, the references, the personal statement, the work experience and the interview training to enable them to put up a strong fight for a much coveted place. Many of these students will have enjoyed support from various sources; switched on sixth form teachers, private tutors or independent consultancies. Why should your child be any different?

Working together with your teenager to ensure their application is as good as it can be is nothing to be ashamed of. However, leaving them to make their own mistakes and *then* fail, in my opinion, would be.

It would be a huge mistake for your son or daughter to assume at the beginning of Year 12 that they can wander unprepared into the Lions Den of applying to UK Medical Schools and stroll out on the other side triumphant. Convince them to prepare for every element of the application process thoroughly and learn to accept help as necessary. Knowing that they need support and being able to choose the best places to get it is a transferable skill that medical school candidates will find useful throughout their training and future career.

You cannot rely on their school to make your son or daughter's application the best it can be. When Molly and Martha told their Biology teacher at the start of Year 12 that they wanted to be Doctors she was excited for them and said a cheery "Good Luck!" That was it. The one and only time she referred to their ambition over a two-year period. Why she didn't show more interest is immaterial. What matters is that *you* step up and provide whatever it is that teachers or sixth form tutors don't offer.

I've already stated earlier that no one in the world will care as much as you do about your child's future. YOU are in a unique position to help your son or daughter prepare their application to medical school. My daughters and I struck a deal early in the application process. They'd revise and I'd research. I learnt so much more than I expected to and countless good things have happened since my decision to get involved with their plans; among them the opportunity to write this book and from that to meet so many talented and dedicated young people who are prepared to work incredibly hard to fulfil their ambitions to be good and caring Doctors. Best of all I've shared in Molly and Martha's joy at getting a place at medical school.

I hope very much that our story helps you and your teenager to achieve all that they deserve. And when that magical word OFFER pops up next to their name on UCAS track that they go on to get great grades and there will be pride and happiness to spare for all concerned.

I won't at this point wish you Good Luck because I don't believe in the notion that good fortune swirls around people at random. What I urge you to do, together with your bright and ambitious son or daughter, is to work hard and see to it that your luck is good.

Is there a doctor in *your* house?

APPENDIX

Contents:

Appendix

TIMELINE

YEAR 11 – GCSE results – are they good enough? For which medical school? Get your son or daughter to visit the websites of every medical school in the UK to find out where their grades would be acceptable. This will be a dummy run but nevertheless good practice for next year. This is also the time to source their first volunteering placement.

YEAR 12 – SEPTEMBER:

- Your son or daughter should begin their regular volunteering. They need a regular session in a healthcare setting where they will have contact with vulnerable people.
- Book early for courses such as Medsim if you think they might help your son and daughter test their commitment to medicine as a career. Also, investigate the alternative free and subsidised courses run by medical schools. These are always snapped up fast so be quick.
- Find out when your chosen schools' open days are held, and book early.
- Investigate early which of your chosen medical schools require which exams. Although you will be about one year early, make sure that you know the deadlines for *both* registration *and* for the exams themselves as soon as possible. Gain as much information as you can about what mark your chosen schools require for selection to interview. UKCAT is a relatively new exam and most schools do not publish a

strict cut off but you may be able to gain anecdotal evidence especially at open days.

- Start investigating BMAT/UKCAT and Interview training courses and pencil them into your post AS results planner for early in Year 13.

SEPTEMBER to JUNE – Make sure your son or daughter are on target for their grades. Some subjects have January modules and these count towards final grades. Remember that many medical schools don't entertain re-sitters without extenuating circumstances. Therefore, urge your son or daughter to maximise their chances by securing the grades first time around. Do they need extra help at school to achieve this? Or a tutor at home? Don't do too little too late.

JUNE – Your son or daughter needs to arrange a work shadowing opportunity in a medical environment. This will be a good contrast to their longer volunteering placement. Double check that you know the registration date of any exams. Do not assume that your school has registered your son or daughter, even if they say that they will. I have heard horror stories of wasted applications where schools had not registered candidates for necessary admission exams.

MAY to JUNE – Get them to write the first of many drafts of their personal statement. Identify any gaps and weaknesses and set to work on putting them right. Does your son or daughter need examples of when they have worked in a team? Or independently? Have they achieved recognition in school or the wider community? At this stage there will still be opportunities to add to their skills and experiences to strengthen their personal statement. Do they have Duke of Edinburgh awards, music grades and drama exams to finish? Now is the time.

JUNE – They need to secure their AS grades. These are the gateway to a place in medical school. Also, if taking the UKCAT, you need to aim to take this by the end of August. The BMAT registration deadline is usually late September, for an exam in early November.

YEAR 13 – EARLY SEPTEMBER – your son or daughter should visit their head of sixth form and get him or her to confirm what their declared predicted A2 grades will be. Cross reference these predictions with their four medical school choices and be certain they are acceptable. They only have four choices and it is <u>vital</u> that they don't waste one.

Your son or daughter should complete their reference pro forma (sample later in this Appendix). Every achievement, prize, interest and hobby that is relevant should be listed for the benefit of the reference writer.

They should re-read the prospectuses of their four chosen medical schools carefully – what type of candidate are the universities interested in? They should provide the reference writer with, for example, evidence of team-work, independent study and communication skills.

Book their place on a reputable interview training and/or exam preparation course.

Appendix

Perfect and submit their personal statement and UCAS form.

Press the SUBMIT button. Your son and daughter must then stay positive and feel satisfied and proud that they have made the best possible application.

Go shopping for an interview outfit – be smart. Make no mistake, it's a *job* interview.

OCTOBER to JUNE – Wait for decisions from universities. Remind your son or daughter to regularly check their junk mail because I have heard hair raising tales of invitations to interview automatically deleting from the junk folders. Then wait some more. I think this is the toughest part of the entire application process.

MAY TO SEPTEMBER – If they have good news and an offer it's time for finance and accommodation forms.

AUGUST – Don't make plans to be away on results day. If your son and daughter have missed their offer by a few marks you will need to swiftly organise and pay for re-marks. One of my daughters had to do this and was lucky enough to go up NINE marks on a paper which clinched her place.
If they get the grades and they are in – it's time to celebrate!

RESOURCES GUIDE

Websites:
We all enjoyed these for a variety of reasons, mostly to share other applicant's trials and misfortunes, which felt so similar to our own..........

www.newmediamedicine.com
www.admissionsforum.net
www.studential.co.uk
www.thestudentroom.co.uk
www.medschoolsonline.co.uk
www.studyingmedicine.org
www.wanttobeadoctor.co.uk

Books
The books we read about getting onto medical were very dull and didn't concentrate on what we all thought was the only issue of any importance in Years 12 and 13 – **how do we get an offer**? Too many talked about the price of a pint in the union bar, accommodation, social life prospects and even future career options that are all of no interest if you don't manage to secure and offer in the first place. At the time of going to press I'm afraid there isn't one I could recommend.

Exams
Remember that there are many books to help your son or daughter to prepare for any exams they need to take, such as UKCAT and BMAT. A simple search on Amazon will provide you with many options. The official resources detailed on the sites are useful.

www.ukcat.ac.uk
www.bmat.org.uk

Appendix

Courses:
These are the ones we tried, ranked in order of how useful they were to Molly and Martha:

Dr Prep Ltd for interview training
Oxbridge Applications
Medlink/Medsim
Gradmed

Taster Courses
These are often run by universities and are either free or very inexpensive. They fill up FAST! You'll find them listed on the following websites or could Google 'Medicine Taster Courses' for a more up to date list

www.lon.ac.uk
www.leeds.ac.uk
www.gabbitas.co.uk
www.uni4u.org.uk
www.suttontrust.com
www.pcps.ucl.ac.uk

MEDICAL SCHOOLS

At the time of going to press, the following universities offer degrees in medicine to undergraduates. Note that all university details, along with *basic* admission requirements can be found at

www.ucas.ac.uk

University of Aberdeen
www.abdn.ac.uk, 01224 554975,
medicine@abdn.ac.uk

University of Birmingham
medweb.bham.ac.uk, 0121 414 3344,
MED-Admissions@bham.ac.uk

Brighton and Sussex Medical School
www.bsms.ac.uk, 01273 644644,
medadmissions@bsms.ac.uk

University of Bristol
www.bristol.ac.uk, 0117 987 7679,
med-admissions@bristol.ac.uk

University of Cambridge
www.medschl.cam.ac.uk, 01223336700,
School-enquiries@medschl.cam.ac.uk

Cardiff University
www.cardiff.ac.uk/medic, 029 2074 3436,
medical-school@cardiff.ac.uk

University of Dundee
www.dundee.ac.uk/medicalschool, 01382 384697,
srs@dundee.ac.uk

Appendix

University of East Anglia
www1.uea.ac.uk, 01603 591072,
med.admiss@uea.ac.uk

University of Edinburgh
www.mvm.ed.ac.uk, 0131 242 6407,
medug@ed.ac.uk

University of Glasgow
www.gla.ac.uk/medicine, 0141 330 6216,
admissions@clinmed.gla.ac.uk

Hull York Medical School
www.hyms.ac.uk, 0870 124 5500,
admissions@hyms.ac.uk

Imperial College London
www1.imperial.ac.uk/medicine, 0207 594 8014,
medicine.ug.admissions@imperial.ac.uk

Keele University
www.keele.ac.uk/depts/ms/index.htm,
01782 583937

King's College London (University of London)
www.kcl.ac.uk/schools/medicine, 0207 848 6501
guysadmissions@kcl.ac.uk

University of Leeds
www.leeds.ac.uk/medicine, 0113 343 7194,
ugmadmissions@leeds.ac.uk

University of Leicester
www.le.ac.uk/medicine, 0116 252 2969,
med-admis@le.ac.uk

University of Liverpool
www.liv.ac.uk/medicine, 0151 795 4370,
mbchb@liv.ac.uk

University of Manchester
www.medicine.manchester.ac.uk, 0161 275 5025,
ug.medicine@manchester.ac.uk

Newcastle University
www.ncl.ac.uk, 0191 222 7005,
mbbs.admissions@ncl.ac.uk

University of Nottingham
www.nottingham.ac.uk, 0115 951 5151

Oxford University
www.medsci.ox.ac.uk, 01865 221689
undergraduate.admissions@admin.ox.ac.uk

Peninsula College of Medicine & Dentistry
www.pms.ac.uk/pms, 01752 437444,
pmseng@pms.ac.uk

Queen Mary, University of London
www.smd.qmul.ac.uk, 0207 882 2240/2243
medicaladmissions@qmul.ac.uk

Queen's University Belfast
www.qub.ac.uk/schools/SchoolofMedicineandDenti
    stry/
0289 097 2727, admissions@qub.ac.uk

The University of Sheffield
www.sheffield.ac.uk/medicine, 0114 271 3727
medadmissions@sheffield.ac.uk

Appendix

University of Southampton
www.som.soton.ac.uk, 023 8059 4408,
Aj2@soton.ac.uk

University of St. Andrews
medicine.st-andrews.ac.uk, 01334 462150,
admissions@st-andrews.ac.uk

St George's, University of London
www.sgul.ac.uk, 020 8725 5201,
medicine@sgul.ac.uk

University College London, University of London
www.ucl.ac.uk/medicalschool, 0207 679 2000
medicaladmissions@ucl.ac.uk

REFERENCE PRO FORMA
You should include:

GCSE Grades
AS Grades
Predicted A2 Grades
Unpaid Work/Volunteering
Paid Work
Hobbies
In School Achievements
In School Awards
In School Positions of Responsibility
Out of School Achievements
Extenuating Circumstances
Reference

We completed the form for their teachers by first listing their grades in the space provided.

For unpaid work the girls listed their work experience at the hospital and the hospice and the charity work they had done sorting clothes for Romanian orphanages. They included fundraising cake sales and charity auctions in which they had been involved a year previously, providing details of which charities benefited and why they had chosen them.

For paid work the girls listed their two-year experience as silver service wedding waitresses. They described how their areas of responsibility and opportunities for customer contact had developed during their employment. Reference contacts were included to support their statements that they had never been late for or missed a shift and that they therefore proven to be responsible and trustworthy.

Appendix

The girls had a good mix of hobbies to write about. They both love sport, took part in various athletics competitions and attended drama classes. They included cooking, reading and socialising with friends.

In the school achievements category, Molly and Martha listed all their subjects and general teacher commendations (given for academic work, behaviour, attendance and punctuality) in addition to noting when they had been Form Captain and had mentored children in younger classes. The girls took part in Maths and Science Challenges and won prizes, so that information was in there too. During their school lives there were several occasions when they represented the school at external functions and they described those responsibilities.

My girls had been involved with family members and friends who had been seriously ill and had been especially patient and gentle with their grandfather, who was mentally and physically incapacitated in his final years. I made a reference to their kind and caring natures.

Molly and Martha qualified as Lifeguards in Yr 11 so we made sure their teacher/tutor knew about that and that Martha had been selected for a Gap Year Commission in the Army.

We also included the names and contact details of two independent referees in case the reference writer felt the need to discuss any of the information we had provided.

Finally we listed the words and phrases that according to various university and medical school websites were desirable in a reference. These included:

Good communicator at all levels
Articulate
A good listener
Shows empathy
Highly academic
Hard worker
Leadership skills
Effective team worker
Ability to study independently
Good study skills
Valuable contributor in-group discussions
Original
Well respected
Cheerful disposition
Responsive in teacher led classes
Sense of responsibility
Handles responsibility well
Reliable
Mature
Able to make decisions
Patient
Determined
Resilient
Good time management
Able to prioritise workload
Copes well in stressful situations
Courteous
Resilient
An independent thinker
Self-Reflective
Positive role model for younger pupils

Appendix

Pepper judiciously with 'e' words – excellent, exceptional, extraordinary, exemplary, energetic, enthusiastic.

You should add to this list if there is a quality your son or daughter has which has not been mentioned.

If the referee is happy to say so it would be a good idea to state the obvious – that he or she believes that your son or daughter would make a good and caring doctor.

Obviously the teacher/tutor won't include the majority of information you provide in the reference. Your prompt sheet will be a useful aide in helping them build a picture of your son or daughters efforts throughout their school career; its purpose is to inspire their teacher to put the maximum amount of effort and concentration into the all important reference and to make it easy and enjoyable for them to do so.

PERSONAL STATEMENTS

Included here are personal statements from a number of candidates who, for ethical reasons, are not the same candidates who divulged their interview questions. Any errors have been left uncorrected, as they were at the time of application. Some details have been omitted for confidentiality reasons.

Example 1, leading to 4 interview invitations

For as long as I can recall, I have been fascinated by the complexity of the human body and the science behind its many systems. My decision to study medicine has been strengthened by my enjoyment of my A-level courses, work experience in hospital, working with residents in a care home and in a hospice. I believe medicine would suit me as I am a motivated, determined, hardworking, and caring individual who is eager to learn.

In the summer of 2005 I went on a month long expedition to Namibia with 14 other people; one of the most rewarding experiences of my life. After a year of preparation, teaching in a rural school, painting the classrooms, making a library and trekking made this the ultimate experience and gave me a true understanding of what it is like to work as part of a team. This trip as well as many others to India, America and Europe, have given me an understanding of cultural diversity and an insight into the disparity in standards of healthcare.

I am currently working as a care assistant in a residential home and I intend to carry on working full-time this year. This experience is making me aware of the emotional and physical needs of vulnerable people and the care and understanding they require. I am learning to prioritise my work and to follow the policies and procedures of the organization. Often just talking to the residents every morning makes me feel that I have made a difference to their day. My commitment and resolve to go into a caring profession is becoming stronger with each day.

For the past year I have been working with physically and mentally disabled children in their school, which has been an incredibly rewarding experience. Teaching them to swim and other skills such as I.T. has given me an idea of the individual care that people with different disabilities require as well as a clearer understanding of some of the conditions that the children suffer from.

From my experience of shadowing medical staff in various hospitals I feel I can appreciate the varied nature of medical practice. In the process I developed an understanding of the pace and pressures of working as part of a team and the importance of multi-disciplinary working. The best experience however was talking to the patients, which I found myself doing quite frequently while the staff were busy, which made me realize the importance of communication with patients and their relatives. Talking of their fears and concerns made me look at my own feelings, values and prejudices.

During my gap year I intend to carry on with a range of leisure activities, dancing- particularly ballet, music, piano, singing, reading and traveling. During my term as a prefect in Psychology and

Chemistry at school I organized a Science Club in which I taught younger students the basics of the subject, outside of their school curriculum. Attending the Medlink conference at Nottingham University where I met other prospective medical students gave me an idea of what it would be like to study medicine as well as a taste of university life.

I strongly believe that medicine is not a career that one can go into half heartedly. All of my experiences thus far have strengthened my conviction that medicine is the right career for me. I feel I am aware of the challenges of doing medicine both at university and as a profession yet I look forward to facing and overcoming them to reach my full potential.

Example 2, leading to 4 interview invitations
Human physiology has always been fascinating to me and whether it is studying physical mechanisms or understanding complex principles, I look forward to the stimulating challenges that a medical degree will offer.
Exposure to hospital life as a theatre support worker at X Hospital, has strengthened my desire to do medicine. At the Cardiothoracic Centre, I have observed the medical and ancillary staff in action, whilst supporting them in a number of cardiac procedures. Interaction with a variety of people in many different situations has emphasized to me the need for effective communication between doctors and their patients, and in addition the importance of excellent teamwork in the multidisciplinary environment of the hospital soon became apparent to me. The need to work efficiently as a team, whilst under high levels of pressure was highlighted during

the emergency operations, something that I first encountered during simulated emergency callout sessions on the MedSim course at Nottingham University. My leadership of a group of 6 students as part of my Gold Duke of Edinburgh Award developed and reinforced skills, which proved helpful in this fast-paced medical atmosphere. In addition to my current position at X, I shadowed both a general practitioner and an occupational therapist, which gave me an insight into primary healthcare. For over a year I worked with children suffering from mental and physical disabilities. This was a challenging, yet fulfilling experience which later prompted me to volunteer to help terminally ill cancer patients at Y Hospice. Volunteering at Oxfam for over two years, has provided me with an ideal environment to practise and improve the skills that I learnt.

My A level studies have provided the grounding necessary for a sound comprehension of basic scientific concepts. Through A level Biology I have obtained an understanding of the mechanisms and functions of the human body. I enjoyed seeing how a basic principle in Mathematics can be applied to find solutions to a complex problem, whilst the statistics modules have enhanced my ability to analyse data and identify trends and patterns. During the Chemistry course, we touched upon how painkillers affect the body, which resulted in further research, culminating in me delivering a seminar on Paracetamol to my biology class. To increase my knowledge in this field, I read 'Aspirin: The Story of A Wonder Drug' by Diarmuid Jeffreys and 'Pain: the Science of Suffering' by Patrick Wall. Reading Robert Winston's 'Human Instinct', sparked an interest into the reasons behind human instinct and behaviour. I keep up to date with topical medical issues, with recent developments in new treatments and possible cures for asthma being of particular personal significance.

In my spare time I have been involved in school plays such as 'Joseph' and 'Cinderella', as well as being a member of the Senior Debating Society. I have represented my school in public speaking competitions and have given speeches on topics such as euthanasia. Last year I also co-managed Junior Science Club, aiming to encourage enthusiasm for science amongst younger students. This required both good leadership and organisation skills, skills which I further honed through my management of Junior Debating Society. As well as being appointed a prefect for Year 7 students, I have also been certified in rapid life response. I am currently a member of Amnesty International, where we campaign about global breaches in human rights.

Having demonstrated my scientific capability through my A-Levels as well as already acclimatizing to the demanding nature of the hospital, I feel that I am well prepared for a career in medicine. In the ever-changing field of medicine, the development of new ideas and the evolution of concepts make this a degree where I look forward to enjoying the challenge posed, whilst excelling in the highly academic and social environment of university.

Example 3, leading to 4 interview invitations
My early interest in medicine was confirmed while spending 2 to 3 days a week having intensive physiotherapy after problems with my knees. I developed a particular interest in overuse injuries

and have since done background reading on several conditions including Osgood Schlatters disease. My experience meant that in addition to being stimulated by the intellectual challenges involved in a science based occupation and the enjoyment of working with people, I am also impelled towards a medical career by a desire to help others as I was helped during my problems.

More recent observation of the work of the medical profession has shown me how much I appreciate the work of the doctors without being 'starry-eyed' about the difficulties. I spent a week at X Hospital where I shadowed in several departments. I was particularly amazed by the technology used for arthroscopy of joints. I learnt that the life of a medic, whether a consultant or a junior doctor, is hectic. On the other hand, I saw that the job can be very rewarding as the medical staff aimed to improve quality of life through knowledge and expertise. Observing ward rounds made me realise that good communication with the patients is essential for their welfare; much of their anxiety stems from uncertainty about their condition. I was based in the elective orthopaedic ward and was interested to see that physiotherapy was used in treatment plans more than I had previously thought.

I also volunteered at the hospital where I delivered food around the wards and learnt the patience needed, particularly when helping those who couldn't feed themselves.

Staying with a GP and observing her work, I watched how she helped her patients emotionally as well as physically; the trust between doctor and patient was obvious. On home visits, her relationship with the community was exceptional. I found that she had a very varied routine, only limited by the number of people in the community.

I have worked in a hospice in X since June for 3 hours a week, which has helped me understand the difficulties of people in the last stages of life. I saw how the hospice works to help the patients deal emotionally with their problems and the amount of time and effort from such a large number of health professionals that goes into one patient. This helps me understand the workload they have.

A couple of evenings a month I help at Mencap, working mainly with young adults with autism, epilepsy or severe learning disabilities, which has highlighted an alternative side of medicine. I realised how little I knew about the mental side of health and have since read The Private Life of the Brain, by Susan Greenfield, which has given me an insight into the complexity of the human mind. I have also attended a medical conference where I heard about different treatments, research and testing into the illness, cancer, as it is not studied in depth in the A Level syllabus.

In addition to my academic interests and activities, I have built up a range of experiences at school and outside, which, I believe, support my application in broader terms. I play the clarinet, and regularly play in concerts. I am a keen sportsman, in addition to having represented my school in the first team for every sport they offer and captaining the hockey first eleven, I have also played at county or district level in football, cricket, and hockey. I have worked part time at a call centre during the past 18 months, which deals with vehicle breakdowns and accidents, so I have learnt to communicate with people in stressful and sometimes life threatening situations. For relaxation I enjoy playing my clarinet, most sports, listening to various types of music and socialising with my friends.

The desire, commitment and passion I have is necessary for the challenge of a career in medicine. I am looking forward to continuing my development at medical school and throughout my life.

Example 4, leading to 4 interview invitations

I have wanted to be a doctor for 5 years and believe that I have the qualities needed. I have excellent organization skills and am a committed, hard worker as well as having a concern for the welfare of others. I am attracted by the way that the medical profession uses science to constantly advance, developing new technology that will benefit people's lives. Science has always been my favourite subject; I have entered competitions such as the Schools' Analyst Competition and completed a chemistry practical course at X University. I enjoy learning and am interested by the continual stimulation and personal development, which is involved in a medical career.

In preparation for studying medicine I spent a week in two local hospitals rotating around different departments, talking to staff and medical students about studying and practising medicine. I gained a valuable insight to the workings of a busy hospital and this experience, combined with two weeks work experience in a pharmacy, illustrated the involvement of different professions in the care of patients. I have attended Medlink, Medsim and X University Summer School and so improved my knowledge about the medical profession. During these courses my observation of a forceful spinal operation and my attempt at the simulated keyhole surgery highlighted the contrast between different areas of medicine.

In the holidays I spent time helping at a workshop for children with special needs. I enjoyed it immensely and was particularly inspired by the genuine kindness and enthusiasm shown by the people who care for the severely disabled. After this I am volunteering to help on a more regular basis. As a young carer for the past three years to my 91-year-old grandmother who lives with me I have learnt a lot about caring for the elderly and also about many of the physical and mental issues involved with aging. This has given me an alternative perspective when researching current ethical issues especially those involving the elderly.

I feel that it is important to strive for constant self-improvement; as a House Captain I undertook activities including assemblies, a quiz night, fundraisers and the production of two house dramas. During my free time at school I am a peer mentor supporting younger students, I am also a helper in a Year 7 Spanish class and I've participated in three foreign exchanges. I spend two hours a week volunteering at an Oxfam shop working behind the scenes and dealing with the public. I ran a Youth Olympics festival that ran for three days and involved over 300 children, for which I was awarded a Sports Award. Although these activities can be demanding they are rewarding. I enjoy working in a team, forming relationships with a variety of people. I have greatly improved my communication skills attending the Rotary Youth Leadership Award, a week long course that focused on becoming a strong, respected leader within a team.

My main interest in my free time is music; I have Grade 7 in violin and play the piano and saxophone. As a long-standing member of several orchestras including the X Youth Symphonic Orchestra I have toured in Germany, participated in workshops at primary schools and tutored a younger student. Music is a major commitment and it has been a challenge to balance it with college work but I have learnt to be flexible and have become proficient at time management. I find sport is a great way to relax and socialise. I play badminton at club level, attending X Training Camp and have represented the school in a variety of sports. I think it is very important to exercise and I have combined this with charity completing the 'Race 4 Life' three times.

All my experiences have made me determined to join the medical profession. I believe I have the skills, patience, tolerance and commitment needed by a member of the health service as well as the ability to work independently and adapt to an ever-changing profession.

Example 5, leading to 3 interview invitations
This year I am studying Biology, Chemistry and Maths. In Year 12 I studies German, I did this because I found it fun, and I think it is important to learn about other cultures. However this year I have decided to put my sciences first. I enjoy maths because there are lots of different ways to attack the same question, and I like how harder questions can draw on all kinds of different principals to solve. I like Chemistry because as you progress you build

up a bigger and bigger picture of chemistry. I prefer to do this using as much practical skills as possible; however I understand the importance of learning the theory first. My favourite lesson is Biology. I find myself captivated by how complicated nature (particularly the human body) is, and how even the smallest parts of our bodies are perfectly adapted for their function. My favourite topics are the Heart, Lungs and the topic we are doing at the minute, the kidneys.

Medicine is a profession that is always progressing, as I have learnt from reading New Scientist weekly. I would like to think that for the rest of my working life I will always have something new and engaging to learn and do. At the minute I am interested in surgery; however I appreciate that there are many other branches of medicine which may be more suitable for me. This gives me plenty of areas to specialize in.

My interests in a medical career led me to do my Year 10 work experience in a Dental Practice. I watched the two Dentists work, sterilized equipment, and helped the nurses. In the second week I took over from the receptionist who was sick. I was pleased to get the opportunity to do this because it gave me chance to do something a little more active. I also spent time in a GP practice where I shadowed three doctors, accompanied them on visits, and did some research for them on abdominal aortic aneurysms. There were many parts of the life of the GP that interested me greatly.

In December 2005 and July 2006 I went to two conferences organized by Medlink at the University of Nottingham where I learnt what to expect from medicine at University. I also learnt some practical skills such as suturing, eye tests, dealing with emergency situations, and keyhole surgery, which was my favourite.

I was a Form Representative between 2002-4 and in Year 12 I was a House Captain. That involved planning and running various activities like House assemblies and the act for the Junior and senior House Drama competitions. Through these I feel I have learnt people and time management skills which I think are essential in Medicine.

I am a keen Trombone player and play with the City Of X Youth Orchestra, with whom I have toured the Black Forrest in 2006. I also play in the City of X Youth Jazz Band and toured Lake Garda with them in 2005. I am particularly proud to have been a member of the Jazz Band when we got to the finals of the National Music for Youth Competition in the jazz section. I play with the University Of X Big Band as a guest performer, and am returning to play with them more regularly this year. I am preparing for my Grade 8 Trombone this year, and also have Grade 5 piano. I would like to continue my music at University as it relaxes me and I believe it is important to have interests outside of studying. I also enjoy being setter in the school volleyball team and have represented my school in various athletics and cross-country tournaments.

Example 6, leading to 3 interview invitations
The large number of specialities and things to learn in medicine make it one of the most diverse subjects. I found this out personally on numerous

hospital visits for a variety of reasons ranging from chicken pox to eye tests. During these visits I also saw many medical teams working in harmony for long hours in an attempt to help patients to overcome illness, malfunctions and suffering. The diversity of the job and the constant learning about the way that the body malfunctions appeals to me.

As a St John's Ambulance cadet, I have learnt a wide variety of skills. For example, leadership among panicked people and how to put into practice basic medical knowledge effectively. I have also found that teamwork and communication are extremely important. I feel that these experiences will put me in a strong position when I enter the medical field.

I attended the 'Introduction to Healthcare' course at X hospital last year. It provided me with insight into the role of doctors within the medical team, highlighting the importance of good communication, teamwork skills and also opened my eyes to the large number of careers open to a doctor.

Shadowing my uncle, who is a consultant orthopaedic surgeon in Hong Kong provided insight into the life of a doctor. I was surprised to find that he spent little time in surgery and often spent large amounts of his time in clinical work, talking with the patients and discussing each case with doctors and the patients themselves.

I spent one month of my summer in India dividing my time between: trekking in the Himalayas, sightseeing and helping with a community project at a local school in Y. At the school, for the children of that town and the surrounding area, a team of us went out to repaint the interior of the building and to do some maintenance work. Many of the children there were keen to help sanding down the walls and painting. The classrooms contained only rugs for the children to sit on, a blackboard and a desk for the teacher. This showed me the dedication that some of the children put into their education to make it into secondary school, working in classes of between 40-50 children. My share of the cost for this expedition was raised by giving music lessons in piano and I feel that I learnt a lot about time management and communication. The job taught me to divide my time between study and work and about communication with people of a variety of ages.

I have also achieved grade 8 in both clarinet and piano and I am currently working towards grade 7 on the organ. My self discipline has been tested by having to divide my time between work, School Orchestra, Concert Band and School Choir, with which I have taken part in several concert tours to Europe. I also play the organ at Sunday Mass in my parish. Learning a martial art, Wing Chun, has also helped to develop these skills.

I look forward to the diversity of opportunities that life at medical school will offer and the chance to become a doctor, working in a team to serve the community,

Example 7, leading to 2 interview invitations
Stem cells can help in the regeneration of body parts and offer hope in the treatment of incurable diseases. Every recent research makes me realize

that this career is so fascinating. I feel that Medicine is a vocation that stimulates my scientific preference whilst also being a profession that would capitalize on my attributes. Having a realistic appreciation of the physical, academic and emotional demands of the Medicine programme, has made me carefully consider my motivations to study it and has only affirmed my resolve to be a doctor. I am well aware of the fact that Medicine requires life long commitment since I have seen both my brother and father work very hard as neurosurgeons Yet it is solely my independent decision to take up this challenge.

The subjects I chose at A-level relate to my career choice. I chose chemistry and biology to aid my understanding of the human body and how chemicals control biological processes. I chose A-level mathematics which has given me the knowledge in statistics that will be required in the medical field. To enhance my thinking skills and problem solving abilities ,I have also taken up the most demanding of the mathematical courses: Further Mathematics.All this to prove that I am a very dedicated person, I hope my hard work is appreciated.

During the summer I spent a month at X Hospital in Saudi Arabia.I worked in the Neurosurgery step-down unit where I saw live spinal surgeries and learnt much about surgical procedures. My duties there involved befriending patients, helping to serve meals and assisting with personal care of patients. I also volunteered in the Radiology department where I observed mammography, fluoroscopy, CT scans, X-Rays, MRI and ultra sounds. It helped me in the understanding of how a hospital is run and

Appendix

functions of different members of a medical team. This work experience has reinforced my decision.

I have also been involved in the school social work committee for a couple of years. Through the school I worked for an institute for disabled people called " Y".It includes people for all ages. I have found this particularly rewarding. It has helped me appreciate that not all illnesses can be cured and that sometimes all that can be done is to improve the quality of life.Also work experience at Z institute in New Mexico State of US helped me to gain an insight about what current researchers are being performed to improve the health system. This improved my inter-personal skills and my confidence to work both within a team and independently.

Last year I won the National Mathematical Olympiad and attended a training camp which broadened my knowledge and improved my communication skills through meeting other talents of the country. I have successfully kept a balance between my academic and non-academic interests by having varied sporting interests, the main one being Badminton, though I also play table tennis and throwball for school. Playing in school throwball team has enabled me to work as part of a team. Also, I am involved in the Duke of Edinburgh Silver Award for the last 12 months which required me to go for a demanding expedition.

Since I am a UK national, studying in UK was my first choice. UK universities provide internationally – recognized qualifications of a high standard. The quality and standing of UK higher education that is guaranteed through the work of various official bodies has attracted me. Studying in UK would also be a multi-cultural experience.

I enjoy playing the piano, a hobby I find very relaxing and have been on a course to learn to play it. My main interests include travelling and Singing. I look forward to involving myself in new hobbies and interests at university. In conclusion, I consider myself to be a well-rounded and dynamic student, with significant relevant experience, and I look forward to the challenges and rewards of life as a medical student.

Example 8, leading to 2 interview invitations
I want to be a doctor as I want to help individuals as much as possible in this world and am passionate about science; I think that medicine is the only career which involves both equally.

Having work experience in a GP's practice really highlighted the variety of people and ailments seen each day, ranging from asthma to heart disease. The way the GP treated his patients, giving the same degree of patience and kindness to everyone, really struck me, as did his impressive knowledge base.

I also spent time in a cardiac catheter laboratory which taught me that although the work seemed repetitive, each procedure varied hugely depending on the patient's pathology. The Outpatients clinic and the cardiac rehab clinic was also very interesting and demonstrated that the doctor's responsibilities do not end when the patient has gone home.

I work as a pastoral volunteer one afternoon a week at a Nursing home, reading to and talking to the patients. This has given me exposure to people who are reaching the end of their lives, and those with debilitating mental illness which has helped me to develop confidence, patience and communication skills.

My decision to pursue medicine has been reinforced by my experience at both Medlink and Medsim courses in Nottingham this year. I was able to speak to the medical students and see what opportunities medicine can offer and I gained a valuable insight into what doctors do and what kind of life they lead. The lifetime experience of having a father who is a consultant Cardio-Thoracic surgeon has enlightened me to the realities of medicine in your personal life.

I love climbing and trekking and next Easter for three weeks I will be part of the X research project coordinated by the Y centre. I will travel to Nepal with the team and I will take part in research into hypoxia, altitude sickness and human performance whilst climbing at extreme altitude. The ultimate aim of the research is to improve the care of critically ill patients in intensive care where hypoxia is a fundamental problem.

This year I designed and led a project to raise funds for an organisation called 'Z' which runs a children's home for Aids orphans in Uganda. Leading this team has helped me learn how to communicate my ideas and has honed my leadership skills because of the need to motivate and inspire others. I have built up a great relationship with the leader of Z and plan to spend some of my gap year in Uganda seeing the impact our money has had on the community there. I hope to be fully involved when over there and take part in their community projects, which are designed to reach out to the town nearby and educate the people about hygiene and HIV/AIDs.

I am very keen on music and sport and I have been awarded my school colours for Basketball and Rounders. Rowing regularly with the X Rowing Club has improved my self confidence, as has speaking as a member of the school debating society. I am the school Sacristan and leader of the Christian Union which has given me a huge amount of responsibility and a chance to interact with people from every year and support them in their difficulties.

I have observed first hand the personal cost, as well as the rewards of practicing medicine, and having spent extended time in various medical environments I know that medicine is the career I want to follow.

Example 9, leading to 1 interview invitation
When I was young, my mother nearly died of an ectopic pregnancy; the skill of her doctors saved her life. Again, when I was hospitalized for Hepatitis A treatment, I received the greatest care and attention, and, as a result of these two incidents, I have developed the desire to use my knowledge and skill professionally to help improve the quality of life of others. This, together with my personal qualities, interest in science, and communication skills played a crucial part in my long-held desire to study medicine. After talking with many doctors, I understand that studying medicine is a life-long learning process, requires a lot of commitment, and that good doctors need empathy, dedication, and teamwork.
After attending the Pre-med Course at X University,

Appendix

I gained more insights into a medical career. This summer, I shadowed a doctor in a GP clinic for a week. I also did a work attachment with the Y Hospital (Indonesia) for four weeks, and I obtained very useful experience of being in four different hospital components: Emergency Units, Labour Units, Intensive Care Unit, and Operating Theatre. I was impressed with how well doctors and nurses cooperated, especially when handling critically ill patients. I saw how communication is vital; listening to patients and comforting them brought me a great deal of personal fulfilment. I witnessed different kinds of surgical procedures, such as Caesarean sections and an appendectomy. The most unforgettable memory was when I saw how doctors, with the assistance of nurses and clerical staff, skilfully performed a hysterectomy to save the life of a woman who had a serious bleeding after she gave birth by Caesarean section. These experiences have strengthened my determination to pursue a medical career. It also makes me more realistic about the limitations of medical practice, caused by factors such as ethical dilemmas, economic climate, and human imperfection. I read the 'New Scientist' and browse medical websites to keep abreast of medical issues.

Before I came to the UK, I did voluntary work in a nursery and I visited an old people's home. I learned how to take care of babies and comfort the elderly. I volunteered to teach Basic English to children in a village primary school every Saturday morning. Helping them was very satisfying and confirmed that I have the patience and the interpersonal skills which doctors must have.

I came to the UK to study A-levels and although leaving my friends and especially my family was a big challenge, it helped me to become more independent, disciplined, and resilient. I learned how to develop my time management skills and how to cope with new environments. I like swimming and playing basketball. I have won many swimming competitions and achieved a first place in a Swimming Gala relay in my present college. I'm involved in the dancing club and have performed in big events held by the college. These activities have given me valuable experience in self-discipline, teamwork, and communication skills. I also learned how to be supportive and encouraging to other members, which can be applied to dealing with patients. My strong sense of responsibility, leadership skills, ability to communicate well, and dependability are recognized by the college by my recent appointment as Prefect, the president of the Indonesian Society, and Lifeguard. I was delighted to be awarded 'Favourite Student' in my previous college. Listening to music helps me relax. I enjoy art and I was proud to win a Silver Award in The Drapers Textile Design Competition this year.

I understand the demands of becoming a doctor. I have fully dedicated myself to studying medicine and I strongly believe, with my motivation, dedication, and personal qualities, I am able to overcome any challenge. Thereafter, I will contribute my knowledge to improve my country's healthcare system. I very much look forward to the day when I first meet my patients.

Example 10, leading to 1 interview invitations
I have wanted to have a career in medicine for many years. I think that it is really important to put something back into the community that you are living in and to do something positive for other

people. For me medicine is a way that I can do this and challenge myself at the same time. I find working with people incredibly gratifying and the feeling I get from helping someone is second to none.

I am currently on my gap year and working as a health care assistant at X Hospital, a hospital for the care of the severely disabled including those with brain injuries and illnesses of the brain and nervous system. From the beginning of my employment at X I realised how little I know about brain injuries. I have found the observation of the treatment of hypoxic brain injury patients particularly interesting due to the very different symptoms patients can suffer from. Although at times it is challenging both physically and emotionally to work with our patients I find it enormously rewarding to know that even the little things I do for the patients make their days that bit better. A smile or wink from a patient who doesn't often communicate makes an "alright day" into a "great day". Before starting my work at X I didn't realise quite how much I would enjoy being with people in this way. I have been convinced by working at X that medicine is the career for me.

I have always been an active member of the school and enjoy participating in all activities offered to me. To this end I was assistant head girl. I was also involved in implementing a mentoring scheme for Year 7 pupils to help them settle in as well as one to support year 8s with reading. I enjoyed my interaction with the lower school and I found it taught me to empathise with the younger children.

I was chosen to sit on the Y ....*omitted for confidentiality reasons....* . At first I found it hard to put aside my personal views on the subjects we were debating but over the three days I grew in confidence and now think it was useful to have to put myself entirely in the shoes of someone else and argue for points that I actually disagreed with. Being on the Y also required that I improve my communication and debating skills. It was often frustrating when trying to persuade others to agree with my suggested amendments and a lot of diplomatic tactics had to be used.

After a stressful day I enjoy reading, playing the piano and socialising to relax. I am also enrolled at a local gym to maintain my fitness. During the winter I try to get as much skiing in as possible and scuba dive in the summer. I have developed an interest in learning sign language and hope to enrol in Makaton classes soon.

I chose to study the International Baccalaureate instead of the more traditional A-levels and have developed a high level of self-motivation and discipline, learning to enjoy study both in groups and by myself. The extended essay helped me to build my confidence when working with very minimal guidance on a previously unknown topic. The IB particularly has taught me constantly to question what I am being told, what I am doing and how I can do it better.

I honestly believe that I will make a good doctor. I have always wanted to challenge and push myself; additionally I am enthused by working with and for people. For me the most important part of being a doctor is being able to communicate and interact successfully with my patients.

Appendix

Example 11, leading to 1 interview invitations

For me it was not a question of *'to be or not to be'* but to decisively take the path leading to qualifying as a doctor. God willing, I will undertake my first MB, then FRCS, then a surgical speciality, possibly cardio thoracic. That's how determined I am to chart my future career. I wish my professional life to revolve around Medicine. I have an enormous zeal and enthusiasm in understanding what our human body is about. Religious and moral ethics, combined with the practical application of medical knowledge to real life challenging situations, fills me with a sense of awe and humility. This is sciences and social interaction working together, testing ones' academic & intellectual rigour and discipline, whilst showing compassion and care.

Having worked in a nursing home at the weekends for the last 18 months I have been exposed to vulnerable patients, often incapable of looking after themselves. This human contact in a social and clinical setting has shown me that medicine is both a science and an art. Patients entered the hospice with a poor prognosis, often terminally ill. This made me realise that medicine is not just about the treatment with drugs but to care for the patient's total welfare, both emotionally and physically. Carers play a vital role in the whole issue of patient care!

I was fortunate enough to have gained hospital experience shadowing my aunt at the National Institute of Cardio-Vascular Diseases in X. I further undertook two weeks work in the Diagnostic Cardiology Unit at Y Hospital. Both these clinical attachments provided me with first hand experience of the importance of effective and regular communication with patients and their relatives, across a variety of language and culture barriers. My fluency in both Gujarati and Urdu were of assistance.

I have learnt that for effective patient care delivery, the various medical professionals have to work together as a team. Doctors have to be able to solve problems rationally, often working under pressure and keep abreast of new developments. By representing and vice captaining both the football and cricket first XI teams throughout my school days, I've built up the ability to work well in a team with a common aim. I also drive, ski and play tennis.

Further work experience in a local General Practice gave me some insight of a GP's wide range of work including all the paper work and the ongoing changes to primary care provision! Here I learnt the effective use of management of time and skills. Whilst there, I helped organise the *Well Men Health Checks* and involved in promoting good diet and lifestyle in the Asian community.

Having visited many different countries, I find that I thoroughly enjoy working with people from all walks of life. Just talking to patients of different backgrounds has vastly improved my personal communication skills. my understanding of human nature and how to connect with people.

I have participated in raising funds for a cardiac machine for a Cardiology Unit in Pakistan, (where, sadly because of lack of resources, I saw catheters being used over and over again), helped with funding for a dialysis unit and sponsored a blind girl in India. I now so much appreciate that we in the UK have the safety net of our NHS.

I have seen two sides to a medical career, one of emotional strain, long hours and the other of an exiting and ever changing career to keep up with the delivery of modern medicine. Medicine is about serious responsibilities and commitment, if nothing else. From all the above I am in no doubt that medicine is my 'raison d'etre'. This is a life long opportunity to continually challenge myself and I hope to make a substantial contribution in the field.

Example 12, leading to 0 interview invitations
Ever since my first chemistry set, science has been a real passion for me. I have a naturally enquiring mind and am fascinated by the 'whys' and 'hows' of our world. On hearing the doctors in our family talking about their work, including the ethical issues involved, I found this interest in science being focused on medicine in particular. I see a career in medicine as a continuing journey of discovery, but uniquely one where I could make a real difference to people's lives along the way.

My recognition of the importance of science came first from school science lessons and then from reading around the medicoscientific world. This interest was reinforced this summer when I won a Nuffield Science Bursary to research toxicology at the University of X. This provided not only valuable experience of research methods and laboratory techniques, but also an opportunity for me to apply at a much higher level the theory I had learnt. Although under direction, I had to work on my own initiative in preparing and carrying out experiments. I also produced a report for this project, and for this I was awarded a Gold CREST Award.

As to the 'human' side of medicine, I have sought to understand this better through work experience placements with a GP in a rural practice in X; at the Y Hospital and through voluntary work with the Z, the charitable trust for the rehabilitation of victims of head injuries.

My time with the GP's practice was my first real exposure to the practice of medicine, where I was involved with not only the medical side of a GP surgery, but also the administration, the volume of which surprised me. I attended several home visits, both with a GP and the local Health Visitor. These visits served to expose the contrast in agendas, of both doctor and patient, when the consultation moves from the surgery to the patient's home.

At the Y Hospital I found the time I spent in the end-stage dementia ward and the hospice unit particularly interesting but poignant: the stark reality of palliative care was revealed to me. I also found my time here useful in seeing the challenges that exist in terms of time and resources in providing a range of services and treatments at even a small hospital.

The experience of working with Z was both enlightening and sobering: here I encountered people who, despite having been seriously injured, would not accept that there was anything wrong. I learnt that this was because, from a subjective point of view, they had not noticed any difference in their personality or nuances. It was only when relatives confronted them that they realised the extent of their injuries. For me, it was a hugely rewarding and fulfilling experience: I worked with patients on a one to one basis to create strategies and techniques to help them cope with their individual cognitive defects. This was my first experience of brain-damaged people and one which further encouraged my keen interest in neurology, and in particular in the 'neural correlates of consciousness'.

I currently have a Saturday job at a local pharmacy. This has given me an introduction to pharmacology as well as helping develop my confidence and communication skills through dealing with sometimes difficult people, such as methadone patients.

At school I was voted Head Student in July 2006, this is a role which has demanded self discipline, organisation and good communication skills, all of which will I believe will be important in a medical career.

To relax I enjoy music- I play guitar, saxophone and piano– and sport, in particular tennis and cricket (I am captain of the school and local team). I also enjoy acting (especially Shakespeare) and have had major parts in five school plays, and helped backstage at another. I hope to continue with these as a part of an active university life.

Appendix

100 Interview Questions asked last year

Included here are a number of questions that were asked last year. Remember that questions which related directly to the personal statement were unique to the candidate and so have not been included here. Your son or daughter needs to know as much as they can about things which are mentioned in their statement. For instance, one candidate who had gained experience with St John's ambulance was asked to describe the history of St John's ambulance.

The 100 questions listed below are a selection of those asked at 20 universities last year.

1. How are you today?
2. How was your journey?
3. How did you get here today?
4. Why medicine?
5. Why this university?
6. When did you know medicine was the career for you?
7. Tell me about a memorable patient you encountered during your work experience placement.
8. Explain how the NHS is funded.
9. What do you believe are the main stresses that Doctors experience?
10. How do you deal with personal stress?
11. Do you believe that the NHS should fund plastic surgery?
12. How do you think you would fit into the medical school and university life?
13. Tell me about the last book you read.
14. What are the three biggest health problems in the UK today?

15. What teams and societies will you join at university?
16. What is your view on Day Surgery?
17. What attracts you to (this university)?
18. When have you implemented change?
19. How would you convince someone to donate their body to scientific research?
20. What journals do you read? What recent scientific article have you read in it/them?
21. What is HPV?
22. If you were teaching at school what topic would you present and why?
23. If you were a body organ, what would you be and why?
24. Why medicine now?
25. How would you tell someone bad news?
26. Do you think the voluntary services benefit the NHS?
27. What are the bad points about medicine?
28. Why should we take you?
29. How do you revise?
30. Describe a time when you have worked well in a team?
31. What would you do if a friend on the course seemed depressed?
32. How are you suited to this type of course?
33. What makes a good doctor?
34. Why do you want to be a doctor?
35. What do you think it will be like working in a hospital?
36. Tell us about an achievement of which you are really proud.
37. Tell us about something that you found difficult to persevere with.

Appendix

38. What difficulties are you faced with when practicing medicine in (this geographical area)?
39. Give us an example of when you have shown good communication skills.
40. What kind of stresses do you think doctors face? How would you cope with them?
41. What would you do/how would you cope, if whilst training, you accidently killed a patient?
42. What can you bring to this course that others can't?
43. What qualities do you think a doctor needs?
44. What is the difference between empathy and sympathy?
45. What methods of teaching do we use?
46. What kinds of effects do you think the social and cultural implications of learning (in this geographical area) have on what you will see in hospitals/surgeries?
47. What are you interests outside medicine?
48. Are health screening programmes, specifically breast screening, justified?
49. Describe work experience undertaken in a health care environment and what you have learned from it.
50. Why do you want to do medicine now?
51. Why do you think you will make a good doctor?
52. If you were given £1 million to make a documentary about something that interests you outside medicine, what would it be about?
53. What is more important to a doctor – politics, law or ethics? Why?

54. What do you think about the government option to stop people getting benefits if they don't attend drugs clinics if they are an addict?
55. What skills do you think a surgeon needs?
56. What are you doing in your gap year?
57. What 3 people dead or alive would you invite to a dinner party?
58. What are the disadvantages of our course structure?
59. Think of a team situation, what went wrong and how you dealt with it.
60. Tell us about the good and bad aspects of being a doctor.
61. What would be difficult about being a doctor?
62. What roles would you have as a doctor?
63. What attracts you to a career in medicine?
64. What makes a good doctor?
65. Tell us about good and bad points about teamwork.
66. Is medicine art or science?
67. Tell us about a difficult situation and how you overcame it.
68. Why do more women die during childbirth in UK than Sweden?
69. Why do you want to be a doctor?
70. What are the biggest problems facing the NHS? Who's responsibility is it to decide how the money is spent?
71. How would you cope with making a difficult decision?
72. What does MRSA stand for?
73. What do you do to relax?
74. Do you think that a doctor who smokes has the right to tell a patient to stop smoking?
75. What did you gain from our open day?

76. What are important skills needed to work in a team?
77. What skills do you have that a doctor needs?
78. Why medicine?
79. What have you enjoyed most/least about your gap year?
80. What do you plan to do during your gap year?
81. Tell us about an ethical dilemma that you noted during your work experience.
82. Are you a team player or team leader?
83. Where does a patient stand in a team of health care staff?
84. When did you decide to study medicine?
85. Tell us about the career path of a doctor, about MMC, exam boards and so forth.
86. What do you do to relax?
87. What is the last book you read?
88. What would your friends say your 3 best qualities are?
89. How do you cope with stress? How does that relate to coping with stress as a doctor?
90. How would you approach a team member who is not pulling their weight?
91. What are the qualities of a good doctor? What are your best qualities?
92. What did you enjoy about your work experience?
93. Do you think having time to relax is important?
94. Have you come across any ethical dilemmas at work?
95. A woman in her 70s comes in with her husband and tells the doctor that she is not taking her medication regularly. The husband

seems to take control and stop her. How would you deal with this?

96. A 60 year old gentleman who smokes needs a heart operation. He is not prepared to give up smoking. Would you do operation? How could you help him to give up?

97. You see one of your colleagues from the course sitting by themselves looking upset, they have been very quiet and withdrawn lately, what do you do?

98. What issues arise from patients being made NFR (not for resuscitation) on the ward. How is the decision made?

99. A 47 year old alcoholic mother, and baby born with genetic defect, both need a liver, which one would you give it to?

100. A jehovah 's Witness refuses a life saving blood transfusion, but her husband is a non-Jehovah's witness and wants her to have one. What should be done?

GAMSAT, UKCAT, BMAT, Personal Statements & Interview Preparation

Our courses, held in London, comprise
Lectures, Handouts, Mock Exam, Extra Practice Questions & Feedback.

mail@drprep.com

01276 29878
(including evenings and weekends)

272 Gordon Avenue,
Camberley GU15 2NU

www.drprep.net